ONE WAGON WEST

BRAD HAINSWORTH

ONE WAGON WEST

To Jackie, Todd, Traci, and Julie for all of the
appropriate reasons

CHAPTER 1

"Don't worry, Jenny," Deborah said. "Ma and Pa will find us soon." The two girls huddled in each other's arms in the darkness of the barn. Their home was burning fiercely. They had not seen their father since a mob of hooded men had dragged him from the yard just as darkness fell. Their mother had run to the neighbors screaming for help, but mobs were everywhere, looting and burning. That was the last they had seen of either parent.

Nauvoo was in flames. It was one of the coldest winters in recent years and although it was after midnight, the low, gray sky was almost as light as day from the burning city.

Deborah Richards had just celebrated her sixteenth birthday and her younger sister, Jennifer, was thirteen. Nauvoo had been such a happy place. Her family and her people were prospering and the new temple was almost finished. But, then, the mobs had come chasing people from their houses and beating them with ax handles and clubs. Wolf hunts, they called it. They shot Brother Tyler and his oldest boy when the two had tried to defend their home and barn. When the mob had reached the Richards' home, masked men broke the windows and threw torches inside and on the roof. The wooden shingles caught fire quickly and the girls had run out into the icy chill to hide in the safety of the cold, dark barn. Their ten-year-old brother, Butch, had run out into the night looking for Pa when the mob entered their street smashing windows and putting homes to the torch.

Suddenly, two men appeared in the flickering doorway. The huge double doors were broken, hanging by one large, rusted hinge, one supporting the weight of the other.

"I seen 'em come in here," one puffed.

"Yeah, they're in here a'right."

The two frightened girls scrambled behind their Pa's big wagon at the rear of the barn, their skirts rustling in the hay. The rear axle of the wagon rested on a large barrel, the wheel missing.

"We know yer in there."

"Ain't that a wagon back in there?"

"Yeah, an' that's where they're at, 'less I miss my guess."

"Leave us alone and go away," Jennifer hollered.

"Hush, they'll find us," Deborah whispered angrily.

"Well, well, Hawky, what we got us cher?" The two men filled the open space under the partially collapsed doors, their features impossible to make out. "Well, now, I think we got us a couple a them Mormon maidens we been hearin' sa much about of late," the other said.

Deborah had never known such terror before. She felt her sister shaking with sobs.

"You get out of here and leave us alone," she screamed. "Our Pa's just out hitchin' the wagon and he's got a gun."

"My, my, her Pa's got a gun, jest outside. Now, don't that give ye pause, Hawky?"

The man called Hawky stepped inside. He was big, and a greasy beard sprouted from under a dirty, red bandanna tied over his nose. Both men stunk strongly of cheap, home-made whisky.

"You stay here in the door," the man called Hawky said. "This here little gal's gonna learn some pretty manners and grow up some in the process."

Keeping herself between the huge, greasy, advancing assailant and Jennifer, Deborah backed further into the blackness of the barn and stumbled backwards into the knee-deep hay which had fallen from the loft. Frantically, both girls tried to scramble for protection further back into the hay, but the giant lunged and caught the hem of Deborah's skirt, tearing it half loose at her waist.

Deborah screamed and desperately tried to crawl, grasping wildly in the dark for a weapon, anything with which to defend herself and her sister. Something stung her hand. It was the sharp point of a pitchfork carelessly left lying beneath the hay, prongs up.

If Butch had been told once, he had been told a thousand times not to leave the pitchfork lying around. Someone could get hurt and....

The man had her by one leg, clutching and grabbing at her. He smelled of sweat and dirt and the stench of back-country whisky was strong on his rasping breath.

Screaming and kicking, Deborah pushed her sister away and rolled over yanking the pitchfork up.

The man called Hawky gave an urgent, choking grunt and grabbed his face. Blood spirted from an ugly gash in his cheek and eye, filling his dirty beard and soaking the bandanna he used as a mask. Falling forward in the hay, numbed with pain, he began screaming obscenities at Deborah.

Blood pounding in her ears, Deborah grabbed her sister and darted back behind the crippled wagon.

"Did ya get 'er good, Hawky?" his companion hollered from his station at the door. "Hawky?" he whispered loudly. "Hawky!" Squinting into the darkness, he stumbled from the door toward the back of the dark barn. Suddenly, he was on the dirt floor of the barn, retching painfully, no air left in his lungs. With all of her strength, Deborah had jammed the end of the pitchfork's long handle into the man's shirt front, just above his belt. All she could see in the blackness of the barn were the whites of two large, startled eyes.

They left him retching and thrashing on the barn floor as they ran out into the freezing night.

It was starting to snow.

CHAPTER 2

All summer long Butch had heard his Pa and the other men in the Church talk of mobs coming and looting their city. Nevertheless, Nauvoo had become the largest and most beautiful city in Illinois. It was a sprawling boom town that had grown rapidly as the Mormon people had fled before Missouri mobs six years earlier. The city sat on a peninsula that was formed by a large bend of the Mississippi River. The weary, discouraged refugees had drained an infested swamp to build their City Beautiful. Now it was a city of fine brick homes and wide streets. The temple, situated on a hill overlooking the city, dominated the entire area. The Saints had built for permanence, but were living on the edge of flight.

Bright and husky, Butch had been raised on the frontier, and he was filled with the marvel of the growing city. The huge Mississippi which crept around the city was a paradise for him. It was alive with all kinds of wildlife. Every chance he had, he would go down to the river's edge and play pirates or Indians or mountain man—especially mountain man.

He and Jerry Tyler had built themselves a mountain man's lair in which they could share their secrets and hide from enemies, both imagined and real. It was a cave in the cutbank among the huge roots of an old oak tree which leaned precariously out over the river. They entered their den between two large roots which protruded from the bank out into the river, and if they were not careful they could fall into the deep water as they scrambled in and out of the cave.

They had hollowed out the bank to make a small cave. It was large enough for two boys to sit in and surround themselves with their prized collection of rocks, snake rattles, an old, rusted pistol, and an assortment of extremely valuable marbles won in combat. They kept their treasured marbles in an old deerskin pouch which hung on a large, exposed root. There was room for three candles which gave them sufficient light with which to admire their plunder and plot future adventures.

Butch loved the smell of the cave. It was, in all of his world, his most favorite place. The humid dampness smelled of clay and decaying wood and leaves. To him and Jerry, it became the very smell of security, secretiveness, and independence.

They would allow no girl to violate the sanctity of their hide-out, and, of course, great care had been taken to keep even the knowledge of such a marvelous place from their sisters. Only Pa knew of the secret place, since the day he helped the two frightened boys liberate their cave. Many times Pa had said he wished that he were small enough to get in there with them. Pa was like that; he knew, he understood.

If it hadn't been for Pa they would have lost their cave and all its valuable treasure. School had let out one hot day in June, and the two boys ran for their secret place. Jerry had reached the river bank first and scrambled through the thick brush to the edge of the bank and down the slippery roots to the cave's opening. As he stuck his head into the dark fortress he heard an ominous rustling. He jerked his head out as Butch slid beside him.

"What's a matter?" Butch whispered, sensing the danger of some unexpected discovery.

"Somethin's in there," Jerry whispered back.

"Aw, who'd be in there," Butch whispered in disbelief. "Nobody knows but us." Then the urgency of the situation struck him, "Our plunder's in there."

"Zactly," replied the knowing Jerry.

"I'm goin' in," said Butch.

"No," wheezed Jerry. "Somethin's in there an' it sounds bad."

Slowly the two boys leaned into their cave. There was a sudden movement in the darkness and a threatening rustle. Both boys scrambled back to the safety of the large root.

"Agh!" hollered Jerry as his foot slipped on the moss. Both boys grabbed for one another and fell into the river.

Butch came up sputtering, his mouth full of muddy, gritty water. "Now y've done it. Ma's gonna get me good. I got m' shoes on."

"I'm goin' home," sputtered Jerry. "Somethin's in there and I'm not stickin' my head in there again."

Butch pulled himself up on the bank. "What about our plunder?" he asked. "What'll we do? We just can't leave all that treasure."

"I don't know, but I'm gettin' outta here before whatever's in there comes out after us."

That thought hurried both boys out of the river and faster toward home.

"I'm gonna tell Pa. He'll help us," said Butch, seizing upon the obvious answer.

There ensued a brief but heated debate.

"There goes our secret, if ya do," Jerry replied in anger.

"Okay, you go back and get our stuff."

"Not me."

"Why not? You scared?"

"You know I ain't scared."

"Then, go back and get our stuff."

"Okay, go tell yer Pa," Jerry said.

Pa had gone back with the boys the next morning with a torch. Perched precariously a few feet above the brown water he had thrust the torch and his head into the cave entrance.

The snake struck, barely missing his exposed arm. It was a huge Copperhead. Pa killed it with the torch. When they stretched it out on the river bank, the snake was over five feet in length.

"We never woulda got our cave back," Jerry observed.

That is how Pa came to know of the cave.

Pa was dead. Inside, Butch knew that for sure. Pa was dead. The things those men had said...the way they had said it...screamed it...the hate.... Butch had never experienced such feelings as he had when they dragged his Pa from the house. The hate in their eyes... Why? Why did people hate what they didn't understand? Why couldn't they let folks be?

Butch's breath came in short, rapid gasps. He had been running for what seemed an hour since he ran from the burning house. He had no idea where his Pa had been taken, but he knew that if Pa had gotten away from the mob, he would have gone to the Temple. In an emergency, that's where the men always went.

It was cold and the dark night had been turned into day by the burning city. The smoke filled his lungs. They hurt with irritation and the cold. Butch stopped to catch his breath. He could hear the excited voices of men up near the temple. If he could just get to them...get help. Butch began to run again. Running from among the buildings along the street onto the temple site, he ran headlong onto the assembled men.

"Help!" he hollered, "ya gotta help me, they got Pa an'..."

Looking into their faces, Butch was stunned. It was them, the men, the black, sooted faces, the round white eyes filled with hate.

"Jest a minute, youn'n," one said, grabbing him roughly by a shock of his red hair.

Butch began to struggle and a scream burst from his throat.

"Hold still ya little runt or I'll bust ya good...ow!" The man danced on one foot grabbing for the other.

When the man seized him, Butch was scared, but he kept his wits and stomped down as hard as he could on the top of the man's boot. As soon as the man let go, Butch kicked his other leg as hard as he could.

"Get 'im," someone yelled. "We'll hang 'im right here!"

Butch did not stay to hear more. His legs began moving almost automatically up, down, up, down.... He wanted to cry, but there was just no time.

"Get the little...."

Butch's heart was about to pound out of his chest. He ran into the smoke-filled night leaving the man he had kicked lying on the ground holding his foot and screaming to the others to get that kid.

The boy had only one place to go now, one place where he would be safe from the mob, if only he could reach the cave. His face was hot and flushed. The blood pounded violently in his head. Several of the men were breathing heavily close behind him. He ran hard but could feel them gaining on him.

Butch darted from the street into the darkness between two houses. What appeared to be the outside cellar door to one of the houses had been left open in haste or fright, the open double doors lying on each side of the black hole. Butch dove into the darkness, his lungs about to burst. He lay quietly as the running men stomped above him into the rear of the yard.

"Where'd 'e go?"

"We lost 'im!"

The men were breathing heavily. Between gasps for breath one said, "Let's quit...hell, he's jest a kid."

Another voice joined the others near the back of the house. "No!" His voice was cold and sharp, "I want that little runt." He was the man Butch had kicked. "I'm gonna skin that little bugger."

Butch could hear the men moving about in the dark yard. A door slammed on a nearby shed and someone knocked over a bucket and swore. Butch knew it would only be minutes, maybe seconds, before they found him if he stayed where he was. The trouble was, it was so black in the cellar, he had no idea where he was. Butch crawled further into the cellar, groping in the blackness.

He was in someone's root cellar. The air was filled with the pungent sweetness of onions stored for the winter. Along the side Butch felt several large bins. He took an apple out of the nearest bin and stuffed it into his pocket. Butch had forgotten how hungry he was and he could almost taste the sweetness of the big apple. The second bin was filled with carrots. He reached in and took one. At the very back was a large bin, maybe four feet deep, filled to the brim with large field onions.

"Down here, "a foot scraped on the top step. "He's gotta be down here, there ain't nowheres else he could be."

Butch had to relieve himself so bad he could hardly stand it. Fear relieved him. He was scared and sick. He knew he was at the back of the cellar and the only way out was blocked by the men.

"Get a torch, I can't see nothin'."

"There ain't one, everbody's gone on."

"I said, get a torch. I want that kid and he's gotta be down there."

There was a scuffle, "Aw, shut up, I'll get one m'self. Don't you let 'im outta there," the voice retreated.

Butch could hear the men arguing as they moved toward the street. "I told ya ta stay put, I want that kid."

The boy knew he must hurry if he were to make an escape. Quietly, he made his way up the cellar steps and peered over the edge of the doorway. Two men lounged in the flickering shadows at the corner of the house only a few feet from the cellar door. He'd never make it and he knew it.

"Here come's Seth with his torch," said one. "Damned if I've ever seed such nonsense over a brat kid."

Trapped. Panic numbed Butch's body. Then he knew. . .the onions.

"He ain't down here."

"Shut up!"

"Well, jest look fer y'r self."

The root cellar was small, no more than eight or ten feet in length and not quite so wide. It was cold and dry and well below ground level. The floor of the house above made a low ceiling and dirt was packed beneath the rafters for insulation. Fresh fruit and vegetables would keep there for months.

The torch flickered and dark shadows danced in the bounteous bins.

"Gimme a apple."

The other's mouth was full, "I tol' ya he warn't here," he slobbered.

Beneath the onions, Butch was sure they could hear his heart. It was pounding like a drum and the men were right next to the onion bin. Suddenly, he felt something on his leg. It tickled and he wanted to scratch it. Butch was scared and knew if he moved the men would have him for sure. Whatever it was started to crawl up inside his pant leg. Carefully, he tried to rub where his leg itched.

"Yeow!" Butch screeched at the painful sting on his leg and burst from beneath the scattering onions in full flight.

The startled men leaped to one side and the torch went out as it hit the damp, dirt floor.

"Dammit all!" one shouted.

"Grab 'im!"

"Come 'ere, ya little..."

"Ugh," one hollered.

"Grab the torch by the t'other end, ya stupid..."

"I burned me bad, Seth."

"Shut up!"

The men lurched from the cellar into the cold night and one said, "I'm gonna kill that kid when I get 'im."

It was starting to snow.

"Seth, leave it be," one rasped. They had chased Butch into the trees at the edge of town.

'Seth was winded now. "Shut up."

"Seth, 'e's jest a damned kid. He don't mean nothin'."

"I said, shut up! Don't go makin' me lose my patience."

The men stopped, breathing heavily. The falling snow melted when it lit on their sweating faces.

"He disappeared over in those bushes on the cutbank. We got 'im now, that river's cold and deep and the ice'd never hold 'im."

Butch's leg hurt him painfully. He didn't know what it was that bit him, but his leg was starting to swell. He was safe, though. He knew that much. He was safe. They would never find him here, not in the cave. Feelings of security dimmed into sleep.

The black water swirled around the ice at the edge of the river and the weight of the new-fallen snow caused the branches of the nearby bushes to hang into the cold water. The river was rapidly beginning to freeze.

"If that don't beat all. That kid's just plain disappeared."

"I dunno, but he sure as hell ain't around here. There ain't been no movement or nothin' fer near onta a hour."

The men moved along the river's edge kicking at bushes and peering over the cutbank into the black, freezing water. A thick skim of ice was building on the surface from the bank far out into the river.

"If this weather keeps up, you'll be able 't walk on this river before ya know it. He's gone. If he fell in, he's dead. If not, 'e ain't nowheres around here."

The men followed the cutbank back toward the town, kicking and searching the brush on the river's edge, their jumbled voices lost in the night and the falling snow.

CHAPTER 3

Leaving their two assailants cursing and bleeding in the dark barn, the two girls ran out into the night. Their world was crumbling about them, as was the world of their people.

From fear and panic the two girls plunged headlong into the quiet, falling snow, Deborah pulling Jennifer after her.

"Hurry, Jenny, hurry," Deborah screamed as Jennifer stumbled, almost falling to her knees, "they'll get us, sure."

Jennifer's uncontrollable sobs shook her straining body until running became nearly impossible. Fright and anger grew into a horrible frustration and Jennifer yanked her hand free and fell to the ground, throwing Deborah headlong into the snow a few feet from her.

"Those men, those horrible, ugly men," the words retched from Jennifer as if she were sick. "What were they doing? What did they want?"

"Jennifer, get up!" Deborah screamed, crawling back to her sister's side, "We've got to find Ma and Pa."

"How...where?" the young girl sobbed.

"I don't know, but we've got to get away from here."

Both girls turned to see what terror was after them. Shadows played on their soot- and tear-streaked faces as they watched the City Beautiful being consumed. Indistinguishable forms loomed and faded as people ran among the burning buildings. It was nearly impossible to identify people from objects as the light of the fires set everything in frenetic motion.

The terror of the city could be heard in the screams and sobbing of those driven from their homes. The air was filled with muffled cursing and periodic gunfire.

As the girls searched the confusion before them for some familiar and friendly form, they saw three dark figures drag a fourth from the shadows, through the unnatural brightness of some nearby burning buildings, and into the smoke-filled blackness. The voices were harsh. A shot sent the three shadows scrambling from the darkness after other victims.

"Jenny, we've got to get out of here and find some place to hide," Deborah said, pulling her younger sister to her feet.

The two were more controlled now and, turning their backs on the carnage they had briefly witnessed, hurried off into the black safety of the trees at the edge of town.

With the ground turning to mud beneath their feet, the two frightened girls plodded on into the snow storm with no real thought of where they were going or what they were doing, their only intent being escape from the horrors of the night.

"Deborah...where are we?" Jennifer whined.

"I don't know," Deborah responded with a sinking voice.

"I'm cold."

"So am I, and my feet are frozen."

They had stopped under a large pine tree where there was partial shelter from the snow and the ground was more solid, if not dry. The huge, old pine bows were covered with the thickly falling snow and drooped nearly to the ground. Both girls shivered with the cold.

"It's so dark and snowy. I wish we could see."

"So do I. I have no idea where we are."

"Me neither," Jennifer sniffed. "I hope Butch is okay."

"Butch'll be fine. He's probably found Ma and Pa by now."

At the thoughts of their family, tears welled into Deborah's eyes and stung her cold face.

"Debbie...I'm freezing. It's so cold...look...my dress is stiff."

"I know. I'm cold, too. At least under these branches, we're out of the falling snow."

"Are we going to freeze here? What are we going to do?"

"Well...we can't go back to Nauvoo. At least not while those men are there. Maybe we should go on. At least it's not so cold when we're walking, and maybe we'll see a house or something."

Deborah pushed the laden bows aside and stepped out into the storm.

"Come on, let's get going."

Jennifer trudged through the deepening snow trying to see into the night. "Debbie, I think I see a light."

"Where?"

"Look...over there...between the trees."

"I can't tell," Deborah said, straining to see into the snow and the night. "How can you tell?"

"I don't know, maybe it's nothing."

"Hurry...let's go see."

In a small clearing, slumping beneath its load of accumulating white wetness, stood a small cabin and some tumbledown outbuildings. The two girls huddled in the snow covered brush at the edge of the clearing.

The door of the shack opened and a dim shaft of light from a lantern fell across the snow almost reaching the girls. A thin, old woman appeared in the doorway and trudged away from them in the snow to a small woodshed. After what seemed an eternity to the two freezing girls, the old woman emerged from the shed, her old arms full of wood, and crossed the short field of snow to the cabin. The shaft of light narrowed and retreated into the cabin with a slam, leaving the two girls alone in the night.

"What'll we do?"

"I don't know, but one thing's for sure, we'll freeze if we stay out here."

"Do you think she's alone?"

"I think so, but you can't tell."

"But what if someone's in there with her?"

"Jenny, what else are we going to do?"

The pair made their way across the small clearing and Deborah knocked softly on the cabin door.

"You'd better do it harder," Jennifer offered, "she might not hear you."

As Deborah lifted her hand to attempt a more self-assured knock, the door cracked open far enough to reveal a wrinkled face against the background of the dim interior. The girls felt the warmth of the cabin on their faces.

The old woman studied the two girls for a moment and then said, "Land sakes, what have we here?" Her voice was hoarse with age. The door opened revealing the warm interior of the dimly lit cabin and the old woman said, "Come in children," taking Jennifer by her arm. Deborah followed.

In spite of its poor condition, the cabin was clean and the warmth of the fire felt good. A reflecting lantern on the opposite wall held a large candle. The floor was of dirt which had been packed and kept swept clean. The dim, flickering room smelled of wood smoke and the delicious aroma of something bubbling in a large iron kettle that hung just inside the fireplace.

"Such a sight," the old woman said, as she led the two grateful girls to the fire. "Setch ye down here in front of the fire and let's get them wet rags off'n ya." The little woman was stooped with her age and the burdens of a long life of hardship, but her movements were quick and sure. "We'll get some of them hot vittles inta ya, too."

Relief and fatigue made response almost impossible. Struggling with her wet clothes, Jennifer said, "We've just come from Nauvoo and it's..."

"I know, child, I know." The old woman helped Deborah pull her wet dress over her head. "They came past here earlier." She crackled a short, ironic sound. "Nothin' here t' bother a selfrighteous Christian. Especially when there's the Lord's work t' do in the Mormon city.

"Could we possibly stay here for a short time?" Deborah asked.

"Course ya can, child. Why else would I take yer clothes off'n ya?" the little woman chuckled. "Here...you two wrap these blankets around ya.

Land sakes, yer s' cold ya look like two purple prunes. Stay by the fire and I'll getcha some nice, hot stew."

The two girls huddled by the fireplace while the old woman swung the blackened kettle out from the fire and began spooning the stew into a couple of wooden bowls.

The blankets were clean and warm and ample. And, for the first time in many hours, the two girls began to feel safe from their terror.

"Come mornin', yer people'll leave, ya know," the old woman said, as she busied herself at the fireplace.

"What do y' mean?" Jennifer asked.

"I mean you Mormons are gonna hafta get outa Nauvoo and out of Illinois all together." She placed the steaming bowls of stew on the table. The delicious aroma was overwhelming to the two hungry girls.

"I know," said Deborah. "Ma and Pa have talked of it for quite some time."

The girls pulled two chairs up to the rough-hewn table and began eating hungrily. "Oh, this is so good."

"Umm."

"Land sakes, I never seen such. Careful ya don't burn ya. It's hot."

The old woman sat down by the table. There was delight in her old, dark eyes. She enjoyed nothing more than seeing her cooking devoured with such obvious enjoyment. "I was about t' give what was left ta the hogs. I got two out back. Lucky I didn't, huh?"

"Oh...yes," said Jennifer.

"If your pigs eat like this, they are better fed than most folks in Missouri," said Deborah.

"Well, if most folks in Missouri'd act as good as them two hogs, maybe they'd be better fed," the old woman chortled.

"May I have some more?"

"Jennifer, what would Ma say!"

"Course ya can, child. And yer Ma'd say nothin' in this house. You'd better have some more, too," the old woman said, leaning across the two girls and collecting their bowls.

"Where is yer folks, anyways?"

"We don't know," said Jennifer.

"Things were so confused," Deborah said, "when the mobs came setting houses on fire..."

"And they dragged our Pa off..."

"We don't know where anybody is."

"We've got t' get back and find them." Jennifer tried to concentrate on her food, but tears kept filling her eyes in spite of her determination to be brave.

"Here, child, eat this and don't bother yerself none now. Plenty of time t' find 'em when there's less confusion."

"Our little brother, Butch, took off, too, and we've got to find him," Jennifer said. "He can't hardly care for himself and he's sure to get in trouble."

"We'll find Butch," said Deborah, "if he doesn't find us first. Butch'll be fine. You'll see." Deborah tried to sound reassuring, but she really didn't feel it herself."

"The road to Montrose is about a half a mile back the way ya came," the old woman said. "When yer people leave, they'll surely go that a way."

"Pa said President Young talked of a place where we'd have to go." Anger and resentment welled up inside Jennifer. "But this is our home. We can't just leave."

"Its not home any more," said Deborah. "Home is where love is. It's not places or things, it's people and feelings."

"But our home...and the temple... "

"Our house is gone," said Deborah, " and everything in it by now, and likely so's the temple. But we've got a home as long as we have each other, so stop crying. Things'll get better, you'll see."

"She's right, child. You have each other and that makes ya as lucky as anybody alive and a sight luckier than most," the old woman said.

The girls talked of their flight from Nauvoo as they finished their stew and mopped their bowls clean with coarse brown bread covered with fresh butter.

"My land, it must be nearly mornin'," said the old woman. "If'n yer goin' t' find yer brother and people, y'd better get some sleep." She helped the girls into two long flannel night shirts and they crawled into a clean, warm bed in the back corner of the cabin. "Watch yer feet, I put some hot bricks in the bed a little while ago. They may not be cooled off yet."

"Oh...they feel so good," Deborah said, snuggling her feet against the warm bundle beneath the ample covers.

Jennifer was asleep.

CHAPTER 4

Butch's eyes opened. He lay very still, not quite sure where he was. It was black and very silent, but the reassuring smells of the cave brought the memories of the night flooding into his mind. His leg hurt and it was swollen, but in spite of its stiffness, he twisted around and pulled himself to the small opening of the cave. A deep blanket of white lay over everything. No sound could be heard, the thickening ice and snow had even muffled the sound of the river.

It was still very dark and Butch knew that he must have slept for no more than an hour. Morning was still a long way off. His muscles ached as he pulled himself from the cave. The roots of the tree were covered in ice and frozen in the river, but Butch managed to pull himself out onto the top of the cutbank. His hands were red and stung from the cold. The snow was almost a foot deep and still falling thickly.

Nauvoo lay silent, the fires dimly flickering here and there as they yielded to the heavy white blanket. At first, the city appeared deserted, but as the boy entered the streets, he could see the shadows of its citizens moving about the wet, smoldering wreckage of their lives The yelling and shouting was gone. Only the shock and disbelief of the gray morning remained. Butch heard hardly a human voice.

The Tyler home was a black, gaunt, skull. The door was a yawning, gaping mouth frozen in a horrible silent scream, and the two windows were now the black sockets of two sightless eyes. He would never see Jerry again, he had that awful feeling.

His own home was gone. Where the house once stood was a tumbled, twisted ruin of charred wood. The fireplace chimney, poking rudely toward the sky, was turning white at the edges as the snow blew around it.

Gathering all of his courage, Butch began pushing, sorting, and searching through the ruins, not knowing what he was looking for or what he would find.

Nothing seemed to have survived the house fire. Everything they owned was destroyed or damaged beyond saving. Nor was there any sign of his two sisters or his parents. The girls were here when he ran out to find Pa and they could have escaped.

The barn still stood and seemed unaffected by the fire and the mob. Butch struggled to move one of the huge doors back out of his way. It was dark in the barn, but nothing seemed disturbed. The pitchfork lay, prongs up, in the middle of the floor, and Pa's big wagon was parked at the rear of the barn. Pa had purchased the wagon in Pennsylvania years ago.

Butch rushed back to the huge wagon. One rear wheel was missing, the axle resting on a large, wooden barrel. The other broad wheels looked as good as new.

Butch climbed up on the front wheel and looked into the wagon box. It was dirty and smelled of accumulated barn dust. Pa had not used the wagon since last summer. The supports for the canvas top were in a heap in back of the driver's seat and the canvas top was in a pile beside them. Outside, a cold wind was beginning to blow, and the barn creaked threateningly under its heavy burden of snow.

Butch knew he had to find his sisters. To stay in Nauvoo was useless. He had seen other families throwing what they could salvage into wagons, buggies, or handcarts.

The boy pulled the large canvas top out as far as he could in the narrow wagon. As near as he could tell in the dark, it looked as though it was in pretty good shape. Climbing over the canvas, he jammed the huge supports into the sockets on each side of the wagon box. Then, the tired boy realized he was still in the barn and that the wagon would not pass through the barn door if the top were on. That's why Pa had taken it off in the first place. Dumb, Butch thought. Besides, one of the large rear wheels was gone. The wagon was useless without it.

Butch climbed down from the wagon and went to the barn door. It was beginning to get light outside. The storm was letting up, but a bitter wind was beginning to blow out of the northwest. Butch looked at the black, smoldering ruin that was once his home. Wedged from the top of the fireplace to the middle of what had been the living room floor was a large support beam that at one time had supported the roof. The burning roof had collapsed all around it during the fire. The small boy climbed through the smoking rubble to the big beam. It was somewhat charred and badly burned in several places, but about fifteen feet of it looked to be in good condition.

The boy's face lit up. He knew what he had to do, if he could just figure out how to do it. He had seen his Pa do it once and it had worked then. It had to work now. Finding an ax in the barn, Butch returned to the house and chopped debree from around the beam. Finally, he had all of the rubble cleared from it, and it leaned long and clean against the chimney. Despite some damage, it was a beautiful piece of wood, but he could not pull it loose. It was stuck fast in its resting place near the top of the rock chimney. To get it loose would take a horse.

"The horses!" Butch shouted, the sound of his own voice startling him. In the terror of the past night he had forgotten all about Pa's two prize plow horses. The boy scrambled from the ruins of the house and ran to the pole corral behind the barn. The two big horses trotted over to him, and the small boy started to cry. They were part of the family and he loved them. The two giant horses nuzzled the boy's head.

Butch wiped his nose on his coat sleeve and climbed the ladder on the outside of the barn to the loft door. Opening the outside loft doors, he began shoving hay over the edge to the hungry horses waiting patiently in the snow below. Climbing down into the interior of the barn, Butch gathered up the double harness and dragged it out to the corral. There, its head buried in the hay between the two horses was the family cow, eating contentedly. Butch had no idea where she had come from, or when, but she was home now and he would need her.

Butch clicked his tongue. "Here Buck, here Nails." The two big horses lifted their heads, and

Butch began the struggle of harnessing the two huge animals together.

"Easy, Bucko."

Butch spoke with quiet authority to the big horses as he harnessed them. He had heard his Pa do it many, many times. Buck and Nails each responded by chewing a mouthful of hay as the young boy worked at the task.

Nails was always harder to harness. The big horse liked to stomp and blow when someone was trying to harness him. Everywhere Butch touched him his skin would quiver as if he were trying to shake off a fly.

"Darn you, Nails, stand still!" Butch slapped him high on his hind quarters and moved the big animal around closer to Buck and hitched them together.

The horses smelled good. It was a warm, familiar smell, and their size made Butch feel safe and competent. The two horses acted as if they needed human companionship after the long night of violence just past. They responded obediently to the boy's directions. Butch soon felt that, with these two large fiends, he could handle any problem. He drove the team out of the corral and around the barn to the burned house and stopped them near the fireplace. Finding a large length of sturdy rope in the barn, Butch shinnied up the big support beam which he had tried to remove earlier. The boy tied the rope securely to the top of the beam and chipped as much of the mortar from around its base as possible. Climbing down and returning to the team, he tied the other end of the rope to the large collars around each of the horses' necks.

"Ho, Bucky! Hup, Nails!" Butch hollered, flipping the reins along the horses' backs. The large animals started forward and the huge beam pulled free and crashed down into the burned ruins of the house, sending a spray of ashes and snow high into the air. The team pulled the heavy beam out into the snow-covered yard with little effort.

Dragging the beam into the barn, the boy untied it near the rear of the wagon and then led the horses to the hay in one of the dry stalls. Outside the wind was rising and the temperature was well below freezing. The boy's swollen leg was beginning to throb.

A block and tackle hung from the barn rafters near where the wagon stood. Butch tied the end of the tackle to one end of the beam and lifted it into the air, leaving it laying at an angle against the side of the wagon. Midway along the side of the wagon a large support strut protruded from beneath the wagon box, securely bolted to the undercarriage and the side of the box. Butch dragged the end of the beam on the ground under the axle of the wagon where the wheel was missing. The other end he swung over the protruding support strut and lowered it until it rested on the top of the strut. Tying the block and tackle to the wagon's axle, the boy lifted the wagon high enough to remove the barrel upon which its axle rested, then he lowered the axle until it rested upon the beam slanting to the ground beneath it. The beam was firmly wedged at an angle from the support strut at the middle of the wagon box to the ground behind the axle which it now supported.

It was not a wheel, but it made an excellent crutch for the large, crippled wagon. All that remained was to find a way to secure the beam fast to the wagon and its axle. The wagon was at least serviceable now, though it would be more difficult for the horses to pull.

Butch's leg had begun to hurt badly and it felt tight inside his pants. Ignoring it, he set his mind to figuring how he could make the crutch fast to the axle and the side of the wagon box. The weight of the wagon would hold it in place for a while, but unless it was secured, the big crutch would eventually pull loose when the wagon moved.

In the tool box near the barn door, he found his Pa's brace-and-bit and several large U-bolts. Bracing himself hard, the boy drilled two holes in the wagon box, one on each side of the large beam. One of the U-bolts fit perfectly and he tightened it down. The other, he bolted over the beam and axle where the two crossed.

Butch stood back and surveyed his work. "I did it! I did it!" he hollered. He was jubilant. Now he knew he could make it. Now he knew he could find the Great Basin, somewhere out west.

It was nearly noon from the looks of the sky. It was cloudy and dark, but the clouds appeared to be lightest near the middle of the heavens. The wind was cold and blowing hard and the snow was beginning to drift.

Butch knew instinctively that now that his wagon was fixed he had to leave Nauvoo. The town would soon be empty except for a few faithful, sturdy men who were remaining behind to continue work on the temple. Butch had heard his Pa talk often of their determination to finish it no matter what the cost. And it would be finished before they completely abondoned the beautiful, new city to their enemies. He had no idea where to go, but he knew the mob would probably return with the night to cause further pain and panic.

His leg had become very swollen. Carefully pulling up his pant leg, he saw that the leg looked bad. It was large and blue with a small red line starting up the inside from where he had been bitten.

The emotional strain of the night and the physical exertion in fixing the wagon had taken its toll. And the poison in his leg made him feel sick to his stomach. He began to feel as if he could hardly move. Laying down in the deep hay at the rear of the barn, he pulled a large pile over him and closed his eyes. Outside, the leaden sky thickened and falling snow began to swirl violently in the wind.

Deborah and Jenny were somewhere out there. He stirred restlessly beneath the hay. He had to find them, he had to. . . .

It was the wind that awakened the boy. The barn groaned from its force and the weight of the accumulating snow. The storm was out of the northwest and the snow hit the side of the barn with the force of thrown gravel.

Butch stirred beneath his cover of hay. It was cold and dark in the barn. He wanted to nestle deeper in the hay, but his leg throbbed and he felt the need to get up and move about. Through the doors he could see dusk was beginning to come on. Then his ears caught the sound of wagons in the street. Butch stepped out of the barn. The street was full of wagons, buggies, and carts of all kinds. The exodus had begun. In spite of the cold, the swirling, driving snow, and the oncoming night, the Mormons were leaving. What possessions they could take with them were in their wagons. Many left as if expecting that someday they might return to find their precious belongings, the accumulation of a lifetime, in the accustomed place. Butch heard one man ask his wife if she were sure the fire was out in the stove. There seemed to be a sad finality to what they were doing, and most knew that they would never return.

"Brother Bush!" Butch hollered at a familiar figure walking beside his wagon in the crowded street. Faces peered from both ends of the wagon.

"Ma, it's Butch Richards," one of the faces yelled back into the wagon. The man spoke the wagon to a stop. "Boy, you'd best come with us."

"I can't...my family's..."

The man cut him off. "Your Ma an' Pa won't be comin', son."

Bush's small wife climbed from the wagon and pulled the small, dirty boy into her warm arms, "You come with us, Butch," she said. "That's what your folks'd want."

"We're moving across the river while it's froze t' Montrose," the man said. "I don't think the mob'll follow us there. You best come with us."

Bush was a tall, friendly man. He had been a close friend of Pa's. Butch liked the family very much, but in his young mind there were now many other things to be done. Through the shock, he knew that now he was at the head of the Richards' family.

"In the barn's our team, an' I fixed the wagon. One of the cows's come home," Butch said, pulling himself free, "and my sisters are somewheres. I'll find 'em..." his voice quavered.

The woman began to object, but sensing the deep feelings of the boy, Bush cut her off, "A man

must do what he must, son." He took the boy firmly
by the shoulders, "We'll be camped on Sugar Creek,
'bout ten miles t'other side of the river."

"Yessir."

Butch turned toward the barn and Brother
Bush's wagon was soon lost among the others and the
swirling snow down the dark, crowded street.

The cold was no longer an enemy. As long as
the river remained frozen, there would be no problem
with the exodus across the river. The wind had
stopped, but snow continued to swirl and twist from
the dark sky. Butch returned to the barn, hitched the
team to the big wagon, and drove it from the barn into
the yard.

"Boy, am I lucky," he said to himself and the
horses. "If we got a wagon, we got a home."

The boy busied himself putting the top ribs in
place and securing the large canvas tarp over them.
"Maybe I should a showed m' leg to Sister Bush," he
said, half aloud. "Oh, boy, it hurts," he sighed.

Nails blew and stomped, eager to join the
solemn confusion in the street.

Butch felt hot and his swollen leg began to throb
again. The small boy began emptying the barn of
anything that appeared as if it might be useful now or
in the future. An ax, a saw, parts of an old potbellied
stove, bits and pieces of bridle and harness were
thrown into the wagon. He even found several large
gunny sacks full of oats and corn. He stacked
everything neatly in the wagon and sinched the end
of the tarp to prevent snow and wet from invading his
new home.

It was getting late now, but once again, the
small boy returned to the burned ruins of the house.
Climbing through the rubble he was nagged by a

sharp pain at the top of his leg. In spite of the cold, Butch began to sweat.

Then he saw it. At first he couldn't believe his eyes. The thing he needed most in this difficult new world lay in perfect condition in the ashes and rubble. He was afraid to touch it, sure it would vanish in a puff of ash if he did.

"Pa's old Kentucky," he whispered in reverence.

The beautiful rifle lay at the foot of the fireplace. The ruins of the roof nearly covered it. Butch pulled away the blackened boards which had protected it and lifted the long rifle from its place of hiding. How Butch had admired that gun. Pa had taught the eager youngster how to handle it and promised the boy that one day, it would be his. Now it was.

Tears spilled from his eyes. He felt as if his father, with pride, had just handed it to him. Perhaps he had.

"Thanks, Pa," he whispered.

The rifle was in excellent condition in spite of its age. Last year Pa had had the big rifle converted to a percussion lock which made it easier to handle and much more efficient.

Taking his prize to the wagon, he placed it under the driver's seat where it would stay safe and dry. Standing on the top of the front wheel and stretching across the wagon's side, Butch hung by his stomach and looked at the rifle he had just placed under the seat. If the rifle were safe, perhaps some ammunition had been spared in the fire.

The pain in the boy's leg was more insistent now and it was nearly impossible for him to walk without the piercing pain.

"I gotta loosen m'pants," he said, half aloud. He climbed into the wagon with great difficulty and in the tray of the large tool chest he had taken from the barn, found his Pa's old hunting knife in its buckskin sheath. First things being of prior importance, the boy strung the sheathed knife on his belt so it hung snugly at his side.

"Golly."

The knife looked handsome with its leather sheath and fringe. Somehow, it too, made the future look brighter.

"I feel like a real mountain man."

Butch took the knife from his side and cut his pants at the cuff, slowly drawing the knife upward. His knee had disappeared, so swollen was the leg, and it was turning an ugly purple, like a big bruise. Sickness began to well in his throat and things started to get dark. The boy collapsed in a heap on the wagon floor, breathing deeply, and trying to keep from throwing up. Slowly, the throbbing subsided and vision returned to his eyes, but the sickness stayed at his throat.

Climbing from the big wagon with a stiff leg was not easy, but Butch returned to the house and began searching for the needed ammunition. He found it where he knew it would be: the bottom drawer of the cherrywood hutch that had stood near the fireplace. The fire nad nearly destroyed it, but not quite.

The horses were stomping. The traffic of the exodus in the street made them nervous. It was cold and the boy's skin quivered and his frame shook until he could hardly control himself. Returning to the wagon, he climbed up the big front wheel with difficulty and dumped the ammunition into the wagon. Reaching for the seat, Butch threw his good leg over the side of the box, but as he pulled himself into the wagon, his swollen leg caught between the wagon box and the seat springs. The boy screamed in agony and fell to the floor of the wagon, the seat spring tearing a large, deep gash in his leg. Butch lay unconscious and drops of blood began to accumulate on the wagon floor.

Startled by the boy's scream, Buck and Nails lurched at their reins, pulling them free from the break handle where they had been loosely tied. Sensing their freedom to move, the two big horses pulled the wagon into the crowded street and became lost in the confusion of the city's retreat, the cow urged into obedience by the rope which tied her to the rear of the wagon.

The snow swirled among the wagons and animals, each refugee lost in his own world of bewilderment and agony. Now, the small boy felt nothing.

CHAPTER 5

The frozen river swept around the city of Nauvoo like a giant, white path leading from the darkness of the stormy winter sky. Dark clouds smothered the river and the city in shrouds of gray and falling white.

From the bluffs overlooking the frozen river and its captive city, the earlier pilgrims could see their fellow refugees slowly emerging from the trees at the far edge of the river, winding their way across the ice and up the bluffs into Iowa. It was a forlorn picture seen many times in the history of the world; but, this time, to those caught in the ancient drama, it held special meaning. The will of the Lord was truly manifest in this new America. West led to the promised land and the hope of peace. To these people, like Israel of old, the world was sparce, not ample. Their freedom, like their food, came at great cost and after much effort. But to them, effort held meaning, and sacrifice would yield abundance, if not in this new Western world, at least in the next.

They were a pragmatic people, too, knowing that if they could only plow, the earth would surely yield, and if they could be left to pray, the heavens would surely part. This was the Lord's land of promise, and his blessings were upon it for those who understood. This they knew, for they had seen their labors bear fruit from impossibility before. How much they had suffered; how often they had begun; they knew how it would end. When a Prophet calls, you follow. The things of this life can hold only so much meaning in the face of eternity. Their faith and rectitude would again yield abundance. Such had always been the promise: faith, work, and rectitude. This land, choice to them above all others, had one promise: the great experiment in liberty. They knew it was so, for so much they had been told. This nation had a destiny which was not to be denied, a destiny made manifest in these very sorrows and sacrifices. From here the word was to go forth and this nation, under laws which forbade religious persecution and insured the integrity of the individual, would provide the abundance which would be the true mark of the world's redemption. Its divine destiny was to lead the world into the millenium, for here it would come forth.

But with the promise of such blessings came the sure knowledge that a people can corrupt itself. The seed of gluttony is always found in the fruit of abundance. Being driven into new hardship was, in a way, a blessing which required a renewal of faith, and each knew his capacity was as yet untapped. Persecution brought renewed determination. Their faith was fixed and immovable, as one had put it. No matter what, stay firm in the faith was the advice. No matter what...no matter what....

The big wagon, with its clumsy crutch, was heavy to pull in the slush of the muddy street, and Buck and Nails had not drawn it far out of town before the two big horses grew weary of their task. With no one to urge them to their usual good works, they slowly pulled their awkward burden to the side of the road and into the trees.

The exodus went on until late in the night, people, wagons, and animals lost in the swirling snow down the road. Snow blew in under the wagon cover and a few flakes landed on the flushed features of the small boy. A scab had started to form on his cut and swollen leg, but blood still dripped in a stubborn fashion to the floor of the cold wagon.

Jennifer stirred in her sleep. The rustle of the heavy bed clothing brought Deborah fully awake. She lay very still, sensing her whereabouts. Then, with the flood of memories from the past night, she sat up, leaned on one elbow, and peered around the dimly lit cabin. The fire had gone out and the single room was very cold. A shaft of gray light lay across the cabin floor from the open door. A slight skiff of fresh snow had blown in. Deborah lay back on her pillow. I wonder what's happened, she thought. Where's the old woman?

A door banged on one of the nearby sheds and Deborah heard unsteady foot steps crunching in the snow outside. The bundled old woman stomped into the room, snow falling from her shoes, her arms full of kindling.

"Land sakes, child. I thought ya'd sleep the day away," the old woman exclaimed.

Dumping the wood by the fireplace, she shut the door and removed her coat. "I'll have a big fire here in a minute. Ya must be starved. It's snowin' and startin' out ta be real miserable like."

"I didn't mean to sleep so late. We've so much to do." Deborah's eyes kept closing. The pillow and warm, heavy bedding seemed so safe and comfortable.

The old woman busied herself in front of the big fireplace, stacking each piece of kindling in a methodical, precise way. "Don't you worry none, there's time a plenty fer all yer troubles. No need to go rushin' into 'em each day."

A small finger of flame seemed to snap from her gnarled, old hand and curl among the wood chips and kindling. The woman stooped low over her work, mumbling encouragement and blowing on the hesitant flame.

"We'll warm some of last night's stew and I'll fry some hog belly," she said, straightening up from her work.

The fire began to work enthusiastically among the kindling and, as the welcome smell of wood smoke filled the cabin, the small flames grew into a cheery blaze. The old woman threw two large, split logs on the growing fire and the room fairly danced into lively, flickering activity.

Deborah could still see her breath, but she felt the urgent need to involve herself. Throwing back the covers she said, "I'll get dressed and help."

"Do as ya like, child, but there's no need."

"We've got to go. We need to find Butch and figure out what we're going to do." She hurriedly dressed herself against the chill of the slowly warming cabin.

"There's little left for ya t'do, child. There'll soon be nothin' left t'speak of."

"How do ya mean?"

"Yer people're leavin' now.   Through the woods, y' kin hear their wagons."

The pot of stew had begun to warm , and the small room was filled with the crackle and smell of frying pork.

"Debbie...let's go find Butch." Jennifer had awakened and overheard their talk. In spite of their night's rest, Jennifer looked tired and drawn. She lay back in her pillow and began to sob softly.

"Come, child," the old woman said, "get dressed. Some hot food'll make y' feel better. After y've eaten, ya can begin workin' at yer life. Y're always happiest when yer workin' at life."

"Really?" Jennifer sniffed, pulling back the covers and emerging from the comfortable old bed.

"Uh-huh...the minute ya start workin' on yer problems, they stop bein' terrible."

"How can they? Just look at us."

"Fer all yer problems, you two make as pretty a sight as I've seen." The old woman filled a plate with hot bacon strips and began filling three bowls with hot stew. "You'll make out all right, jest wait and see."

With the increasing warmth of the room and the delicious smell of the food, the girls began to feel more cheerful.

"We'll find Butch today," Deborah said. "After all, he can't have gone far, and everybody knows him."

"Yeah," Jennifer agreed, through a mouthful of food.

"We can start looking for him at home, and..."

"Debbie," Jennifer slumped over her food, "I just can't bear to go back there. "

"Here, child, eat these vittles. They'll make y' feel better," said the old woman as she cluttered the old table with bowls and dishes of food.

"We'll look for him along the road first," said Deborah. "I'll bet we find him before we get home."

By the time the girls had finished eating and had gotten fully dressed, it was late afternoon.

"You've been so kind to us. I don't know what we'd have done if we hadn't stumbled on to your cabin."

"Oh, yes," Jennifer agreed. "How can we ever thank you?"

"Well, about the time ya think yer world's come ta' a end and ya haven't got a friend in the world, somebody opens a door and lets ya in. That's all I done." The old woman put out her hand and touched Jennifer on the cheek. "Y' must fill yer soul with wonder, child. Yer about t' have a great adventure. Be happy and live up t' it."

Tears blurred Jennifer's eyes and she threw her arms around the old woman's neck, burying her tears in the old, gray hair. The two held each other, each drawing strength from the other's arms, each filling different needs, each facing an uncertain future.

Deborah leaned down and kissed the old woman on her damp, wrinkled cheek.

"Please come with us," the words seemed to come from nowhere. "We can all go to the west."

Jennifer released her tight hold and said, "Oh, yes. Please come. We can make it together."

The old woman sat down and seemed to grow smaller as she slumped in the chair near the table.

"Child...this old body's made its last trip anywheres. This here's my home, such as it is. You

go on from here and fill the world with yer dreams."
She wiped her eyes with her shawl and said, "Now,
the two of you had best be goin' er ya'll never find yer
brother."

Reluctantly, the girls left the warmth of the old
woman and her cabin.

"I keep feeling like parts of me are always
being torn away," sniffed Jennifer. "Ma and Pa,
Butch, our home, Nauvoo, and now this. When'll it
stop?"

"I don't know," Deborah sighed, "probably
never."

The falling snow was growing deep and the two
girls trudged through the trees toward the distant
jumble of the exodus.

"What'll she do all by herself?" Jennifer
asked.

"I don't really know."

"That wonderful old woman." Jennifer stopped and looked back at the burdened old cabin.
"She's so alone...so fragile."

"She's not really alone," said Deborah. "She's
where she wants to be. She's loved a husband and
raised a family there." Deborah's voice wavered.
"Maybe she's the lucky one. She can stay where her
life has been. Wherever she looks she sees the faces
of her loved ones. Their memories are in the table,
the chairs, the fireplace, the old clothes and bedding,
the dishes, everywhere, in everything. Leaving
there would be a terrible cruelty to her."

"Oh, Debbie," Jennifer cried, "that's beautiful.
It is true, isn't it?"

Swallowing their emotions, the two girls
turned and continued their struggle through the snow
into the woods. Taking Jennifer by the hand,

Deborah concentrated on the deep snow immediately in front of them. The dying light made the going even more difficult.

"Debbie, what're we going to do?" Jennifer began to feel overwhelmed and her youthful resolve began to weaken.

"We're going to find Butch and we're going to go on, that's what we're going to do."

"Oh...it seems almost too hard. What's the use?"

"Nothing seems very easy anymore, but..."

Nails stomped and blew as the two familiar figures emerged from the trees and falling snow.

The two girls screamed with fright as they looked up into the faces of the two animals.

Then Jennifer cried, "It's Nails and Buck...and look, there's the cow in back of the wagon. Oh...how wonderful."

The two grateful girls threw their arms around the necks of the two large horses. Then Deborah stumbled through the snow and climbed to the seat of the big wagon.

"Oh...Butch!" she exclaimed, struggling to his side in the wagon.

Jennifer climbed up the big front wheel. "What's the matter?"

"Butch? Butch!" Deborah sat on the wagon floor holding her little brother in her arms, trying to arouse him.

The boy moaned and mumbled and then relaxed again.

"Oh, Debbie, look at his leg."

Butch winced in his deep sleep as Jennifer touched the painfully swollen and infected leg.

"Oh, Debbie, look...it's cut and bleeding," Jennifer said, as she wiped the blood from her hand onto her skirt.

"Here...you hold 'im and let me see."

The leg was swollen stiff and a dark, ugly purple.

"What are we going to do?" Deborah said, half to herself. Reaching up under her skirt, she began ripping her pettycoat.

"What're you doing?"

"I'm making some sort of bandage," she said, as she began tearing the material into a long, wide strip.

Deborah bandaged the leg as best she could and said, "It's full of poison...we've got to get 'im to a doctor."

"Oh, Debbie, he's lost so much blood. Just look at the floor of the wagon."

"Here...help me make 'im a little more comfortable. Pull these grain sacks back here and we'll cover 'im with this old blanket."

"Debbie...that blanket used to be on Ma and Pa's bed, remember?"

The two girls worked feverishly to make their little brother as comfortable as possible.

"Where'll we find a doctor now?"

"I don't know, but we'd best be about it, it's getting almost too dark to try to move the wagon."

Deborah climbed to the wagon seat only to find that the reins had fallen over Buck's rump to the ground on the right side of the wagon. The road was almost empty now, and Nauvoo lay silent in the dark and the cold.

"We've got to move on, though. The mob's likely to return and we're still too close to home."

As soon as she mentioned home and the mob, she wished she hadn't.

"Oh, Debbie, they won't find us, will they?" Jennifer said.

"Don't worry, we'll be long gone when they show up, if they do again," Deborah yelled from the ground outside. Her voice was filled with a reassurance she did not feel. She knew they had already been too long. "The old woman told us the Saints would cross the river to Montrose, and...oh...Jennifer look at this wagon."

Jennifer stuck her head around the opening of the canvas cover and looked to where Deborah now stood at the rear of the wagon.

"Oh, my goodness, what's happened? The wheel's gone."

Deborah tapped hesitatingly at the huge brace and then gave it a kick. "I don't know, but it seems sturdy enough." She kicked it once more. "I don't remember Pa fixing this old wagon, do you?"

"No, I don't. You don't suppose Butch could have done that, do you?"

Deborah climbed back up beside Jennifer in the box seat. No, he's too little and that's a solid job," she said pulling the reins tight. "It looks like Pa did it...or the blacksmith."

Deborah gave the reins a hard flip. "Get up Buck...back...back..." The horses grudgingly backed in their traces, but the wagon refused to budge. "Back Nails...back Buck!" Deborah, said, flipping the reins again. "What's the matter, anyway?"

"Maybe it's the big stick where the wheel should be."

"Here...hold these," Deborah said, handing the reins to her sister.

Deborah climbed down and walked to the back of the wagon. The huge beam was wedged deeply into the snow and frozen ground. A smaller piece might have broken under the strain. She mounted to the seat, and said, "Its a good thing the ground's frozen or we might really be stuck."

"Why?"

"The end of that crutch would have gone right down into the ground when I tried to back the wagon out of here. It might have even snapped off."

Deborah took the reins from her sister and gave the two big horses a slap. "Let's see if we can get through these trees and out onto the road...ho, Buck...move Nails!" The large horses, weary of the cold, strained into their harness and the wagon slowly moved forward.

"It's moving," Jennifer said, with enthusiasm, "it's moving."

"Yes, if that brace is just as sturdy as it looks," Deborah said, with mounting hope.

Knowing instinctively that they were to return to the road, the two big draft animals carefully dragged the large wagon between the snow covered trees to the roadway.

The exodus of hundreds of wagons and thousands of feet throughout the day had earlier turned the road into a muddy, slushy path of brown muck, but with the coming of night and the falling temperature, it had become a rutted highway of ice and snow.

"I don't even know where Montrose is," Deborah said.

"Me neither."

"I remember Pa talking about it, though, and from what I can see of the road in the dark, the Saints must have gone this way."

The girls' voices jumped unevenly as the struggling horses pulled the crippled wagon over the rough, frozen road.

The wagon struggled around the bend in the road and the wide, frozen expanse of the Mississippi River spread before them in the night.

"Do ya suppose it's frozen enough t' carry us?" Jennifer asked between tight jaws and chattering teeth.

"It must...look at the tracks across the ice. It looks like everybody went this way earlier."

On the ice, the going was not quite so rough, and the hesitant horses gained a little more speed with their increasing confidence in the stability of the frozen river beneath them. The snow was falling thicker now.

"Debbie?"

"What?"

"I wish we didn't have to call her that."

"Call who what?"

"Call the old woman, 'old woman'."

Slowly, the wagon left the shore far behind and became enveloped in the darkness and falling snow.

"You know...I never even thought to ask her her name."

"Neither did I. And, now, I feel like I'm leaving behind someone close. Someone I love." Jennifer shivered. "I'm so cold."

"We'll be warm again...soon."

***

A dozen men emerged from the woods and stood at the edge of the river where the road went out onto the ice.

"Look't out there."

"Where?"

"Out there," one of the men said, pointing with obvious irritation. "That's a wagon out there, ain't it?"

"Wheres...I don't see nothin'. It's snowin' s' hard, how ken a body tell, with all that snow 'n' ice 'n' all?"

"Yeah," another agreed, "cummon, let's go."

"I tell ya, there's a wagon out there on the river ice."

"No, there ain't, and if'n it was, it wouldn't be worth goin' after. Now let's get int' town and have us a wolf hunt an' some real fun."

The group turned back toward Nauvoo and disappeared into the snowy darkness. One man swore and reluctantly turned to catch up with the others.

CHAPTER 6

The doctor leaned back from the boy's bed, "He needs lots of rest."

"What's going to happen to 'im?" asked Jennifer.

"He'll be all right with lots of rest and good food."

"He'll be all right, then?" Deborah reaffirmed anxiously.

"Yes, but he could have lost his leg," said the doctor, as he struggled from Butch's bed at the rear of the wagon toward the opening at the front, "but the bleeding from that gash probably saved it...and possibly his life."

Following the doctor, Deborah and Jennifer climbed down from the wagon into the snow and mud of Sugar Creek.

"What happened to him?" Deborah asked, struggling to keep her dress from getting any more muddy and wet than it already was.

"It was some kind of spider bite. At least that's what it looks like."

"Ugh," exclaimed Jennifer, with a look of disgust on her pretty face.

"How awful. Where could he have gotten it?"

"No tellin' where kids'll crawl around now days. Things are so upset." The doctor started off toward a neighboring tent, "Keep 'im warm and give 'im lots of hot broth. I'll be back tomorrow."

"But doctor, when are the Saints going to break camp and start west?"

The old doctor turned in the snow, "President Young isn't here yet and probably won't be for another week or so, but I suspect it'll be shortly after that." The doctor turned back toward the tent, "I don't even know if he knows himself at this point."

"Then will we be able to go, too?" called Jennifer after the retreating man.

"Let's see what the next few days bring, and then we'll decide," the doctor answered, stopping at the opening of the shabby tent. "He's been a mighty sick young fella. We don't want to hurt 'im more. Remember...lots of broth." The doctor dipped out of sight into the snow covered tent.

The two girls stood in the mud and snow and surveyed the wretched scene before them. Sugar Creek was a miserable clutter of covered wagons, tents, and buggies. The Saints were awaiting the arrival of their prophet with much hope, but scant assurance for the future. A city, once beautiful and comfortable, had been destroyed and its citizens driven onto a hostile frontier unprepared for the hardships that awaited them.

"Debbie, just look at us. Where is anyone expected to get broth?" Jennifer said, surveying the miserable scene before her.

"We'll make out okay."

"No," Jennifer sighed in despair, "I mean the Mormons...all of us from Nauvoo. What did we ever do to deserve something like this?"

"Nothing, except try to be free and speak out for human liberty. I guess the folks in Missouri don't much care for that right now."

"Yes, but we're not slaves."

Deborah climbed back up into the wagon, "We are now...to bigotry, and we will be until we get out of here."

The next day dawned with a cold wind driving the snow under the wagon and up through the cracks between the floor boards. The clouds were a sodden, dark gray and folded low overhead giving the day a dull light which cast no shadow.

Jennifer rolled over under the blankets and bundles they had assembled as bed coverings. "Oh...it's cold. I wish we could build a fire." Her back and hips hurt from sleeping on the hard wagon floor, and she ached all over. Jennifer nudged her sister, "How're we going to build a fire to cook?"

"I don't know. I guess we'll have to try to build one under the wagon, if we can scrape the snow away," Deborah said, leaning over and feeling her brother's forehead. "We haven't very much to cook, anyway."

Jennifer poked a large burlap bag near her head. "Looks like we have some wheat or oats. We can melt some snow and make hot cereal."

"One good thing about the cold, I think it has helped to break Butch's fever," Deborah said, pulling herself free of the bedding. "Let's get up and see what has to be done."

The frigid morning air penetrated her body as she hurriedly dressed. By the time she pulled her shoes on, her body was shaking almost without control. "We've got to figure out how to have a fire," she chattered, "and then we've got to find a way to make plenty of hot broth for Butch."

"I wonder where we could get a couple of chickens," said Jennifer, as she finished dressing.

"Dreamer."

The two girls climbed from the wagon. The snow was much deeper and had drifted into piles around the wagon's wheels.

"Oh, Debbie, with this wind we'll never be able to keep a fire under the wagon. Look what the snow's done."

"I know. Let's see if we can..."

"Deborah Richards!" Sister Bush called as she trudged through the snow toward the wagon. "Jennifer!"

"Oh, Sister Bush..." Jennifer responded with gratitude.

"Why, you two poor things, you're gonna freeze, the way you're dressed. Where's Butch? Did 'e find ya?"

"Well...no...we sort of found him," Jennifer responded.

"Yes, and he's in the wagon and very sick."

"Somehow," Jennifer said, "in all of the confusion, he got 'imself bitten by a poisonous spider or something. Doc said he's lucky he's not dead or lost 'is leg or something."

"Well...we'll fix 'im good as new," the small woman said, putting her arms around the two girls. She looked drawn and tired. "You two come with me to our wagon. Brother Bush has fixed us a lean-to by the wagon where we have a fire and a place for the horses."

"But Butch..."

"Don't you bother about him. Brother Bush'll move yer wagon an' all over by us and we'll start fixin' 'im up right away."

The Bush's camp was snug against the leeward side of a small, protective bluff. A lean-to had been built from the side of the wagon to the bluff and covered with brush. Nearby was a small, sheltered corral for the animals.

Mrs. Bush was a tidy woman and her camp was as clean, orderly, and snug as could be expected under the miserable conditions which surrounded them. To the two cold girls, it seemed cozy and warm compared to their own circumstances.

"We've got plenty of food," the woman said, as she suspended two large, black kettles from an iron frame secured above the fire. "Just like the Prophet said, Brother Bush figures we've got enough to last us over a year, or 'till we get where we're goin, more'n likely. We expect you three to stay with us now 'till we get t' wherever Brother Brigham leads us."

"But we can't do..."

"Yes, ya can," she lay two dressed, plump chickens on a rude table suspended from the side of the wagon. "Jennifer, you come and help me cut these up. We'll boil 'em to make broth for Butch and eat the rest."

"Where did you get these?" Jennifer asked in wonder.

"Never you mind, there aren't many of 'em, but these two will be put to good use."

The little woman looked drawn and haggard and her usually quick movements began to slow.

"Deborah, honey...you come and help her. I've got to sit down."

"You look all done in," Jennifer said, as Deborah helped the small woman to a makeshift chair near the fire.

"Well...I helped the doctor last night...oh, thank you...this feels good. That poor man delivered nine babies last night."

"Nine babies..."

"Can you imagine? I stayed with 'im as long as I could. One little one was born under a tent made out of blankets and tree bark. Several of the sisters had to hold pots and pans to catch the water seeping through the top of the tent so the mother wouldn't get soaked as she gave birth." The little woman sat with her gaze fixed on the fire. "He finally sent me home," she sighed. "That's when I saw you two girls."

It was not long before the delicious aroma of the boiling chickens began to fill the air. The atmosphere soon began to improve and the two girls felt more cheerful.

"Here comes Brother Bush with our wagon now."

"Yes. He'll pull it up close to ours. Your horses look like they're about to drop, but a little shelter and some feed 'll perk 'em up, just like us."

Brother Bush stomped in under the lean-to, the snow falling from his pants and boots. "Them horses of yours were about froze. They'll be all right now, though."

"Oh, we're so grateful for your help. We're lucky we didn't all freeze." Jennifer got up from her warm spot by the fire. "I'd better check on Butch," she said.

"He's still asleep. I checked on 'im before I moved the wagon. He's all bundled up, so I don't think he's cold." Brother Bush stood with his back to the fire. "Poor little fella looks all done in."

Brother Bush turned and began briskly rubbing his hands over the fire and said, "Speaking of kids, where's all of ours?"

"Asleep in the wagon, I hope. Please don't wake them yet. I don't think I could stand it."

"You look dead tired."

"I am...purely."

"Why don't y' crawl up in the wagon and get some rest," Bush said, rubbing his wife's neck and back.

"Yes, " said Deborah, "we'll finish with this broth, and I'll make some dumplings for tonight. A whole pot full."

"Now, that broth is for Butch..."

"I know, but we can make it stretch," said Deborah. "We'll fill it with onions and whatever else we can find to make do."

"Mr. Bush, where's some flour and stuff?" asked Jennifer.

"I'll getcha what y' need," the big man said, as he turned toward the wagon.

"It's all right there in the back of the wagon," the little woman said, struggling from her seat.

"Now, you set still..."

"I'm going to help you with the things they'll need," she insisted, pushing her objecting husband away, "and then maybe I will try to get a little rest."

"What was that?" Jennifer asked.

"What?"

"I thought I heard..."

"Debbie...Jennie...where are ya?" the weak voice could hardly be heard coming from the other wagon.

"It's Butch," Jennifer squealed.

"Yes...it is," Deborah said, as the two girls hurried toward their wagon.

Butch was sitting half up, leaning on his elbows, "I'm hungry."

"Oh, Butch," said Deborah, with relief as she sat down on the floor of the wagon next to her brother. The sudden relief from the tension, fear, and worry of the past few days left her feeling weak.

"I'm hungry," mimicked Jennifer, "is that all you've got to say after all the trouble you've caused."

"Oh, Butch..." Deborah took his head in her hands and kissed his now cool forehead.

"Whatcha doin' that fer?" he objected.

"We found you in the wagon on the road out of town," Deborah continued, unperturbed, "and we've come on here to Sugar Creek."

"Oh...yeah." The boy sank back on his pillow, the nightmares of the past days flooding back into his young mind. "Where's Ma and Pa?" he half whispered.

"They're gone, Butch. We don't know where."

Jennifer sank to her knees, her face buried in her hands, "Gone...that's all, and won't be back, Butch. We're all alone...just us three."

"Jennifer, please don't," Deborah said, gently stroking her sister's hair. Wiping the tears from her own eyes she said, "That won't help us, it'll only make things worse." She took her brother and sister each by the hand, the three lost for a brief moment in their own thoughts of the past.

It would have been easier to cry, but Butch sensed what had to be done, "But where's Brother Bush I was 'posed t' find 'im here an'..."

"I'm right here, boy." The tall man was standing on one of the spokes of the wagon wheel and leaning into the wagon where he could see the small boy and his sisters. "Yer sisters found us and we're fixin' t' make things right fer the big move west."

"West? Ya mean we're finally gonna go west?" I can..." Excitement rose within the boy and he began to get up, eagerly responding to the idea.

"Now, Butch, you..."

"Ugh...do I feel sick," the boy said, falling back on his makeshift bed, his head spinning and his face an ashen white. "I think I'm gonna throw up."

"Don't do that," Jennifer said, sufficiently recovered to continue scolding her little brother. "How would we clean a mess up in here?"

"Jennifer!"

"Butch, you lay still. You've been mighty sick and you need lots of rest." Deborah pulled the covers up over his exposed chest. "The last thing we need is for you to catch your death of pneumonia while we're trying to get you better."

"You lay still, boy. Time's a plenty fer you an' me t' get things t'geather, hear?"

"Yessir." Butch felt in no condition to argue further. "But, I'm still hungry."

"How can you be hungry and sick at the same time," asked Jennifer, knowing full well that with her little brother it was not only possible but altogether probable.

"I'm hungry sick."

Deborah felt his forehead. "There's a hot pot of
chicken and dumplings cooking right now."

"Chicken and dumplings...ugh."

"Its good for ya, and besides," chimed in
Jennifer, "the Doc says we're t' fill ya with lots of hot
broth, and that's exactly what we're going t' do, so
there."

Butch was too tired for further argument.
"Okay." Darkness welled up and he slept.

"He's gonna be all right, now. You can tell,"
said Bush. "A day or two and he'll be all over the
place with my young'ns."

"I think he's changed, Brother Bush." Deborah
looked fondly at her little brother. "He's growing
up...too fast."

"I expect so."

"Let's get back to that stew," said Deborah.

The two girls moved quietly to the front of the
wagon, their ample skirts rustling as Brother Bush
helped them to the ground.

"He used to trouble Pa something awful about
the west," said Deborah, holding her skirts above the
snow and mud as the three made their way back to
Bush's lean-to. "He always talked about being a
mountain man. A mountain man," she chuckled.
"I guess he's going to get his chance now."

"Well," said the big man, stroking his bristled
chin, "we'll see what can be done to help 'im. Good
mountain men aren't all that plentiful, I expect."

CHAPTER 7

Jasper Pughsey was a man to reckon with. In fact, in the parlance of the West, he was a bad man. Not bad in the sense of being a thief or murderer, but a highly skilled mountain man, skilled in the arts and tools of survival, and unafraid to use them. One did not trifle with Jasper Pughsey without giving a great deal of thoughtful consideration to the likely outcome.

Under his buckskin shirt, Jasper carried a knife, his Green River, sheathed between his shoulder blades. Many was the careless assailant who found himself face down in the dirt, the deadly Green River at his throat because he had allowed Jasper to scratch an itch at the back of his neck.

No one knew where he came from. The Crow said he was the son of a huge grizzly that had a sore tooth all while she carried him. That is probably as close to the truth as one would ever get. His age was a matter of debate, but his physical strength, his accuracy with his Hawkin long rifle, his wilderness savvy, and his character were not.

Jasper Pughsey loved the West—anywhere in the West, from the stark but beautiful deserts and canyons of the southwest, to the rugged Rocky Mountains, to the pine forests of the great northwest. In the wild he was at home.

It was July and time for rendezvous. The yearly rendezvous of the mountain men was held at Bear Lake on what would one day become the Utah-Idaho border. Trappers, mountain men, Indians, and various assortments of footloose adventurers journeyed hundreds of miles on foot, by horse, or by pack train to join in the revelry and to trade for the valuable furs, knives, guns, lead and powder, and general foofuraw brought to the rendezvous by agents of the large trading and fur companies.

If one was not killed in trying to get there, his chances of staying healthy after his arrival were not much better. Still, they came and drank and ate and traded and drank and fought and chased squaws and drank and loved it. Many came rich and left bereft of even their pants; others came with nothing and through superior strength or cunning or both, left comparatively rich.

Jasper had left his camp on the Bitterroot nearly three weeks earlier headed south for Bear Lake. He had spent the winter trapping the Bitterroot and the better areas of the north central Rockies. On his three pack horses were huge bundles of precious fur. Jasper had two objectives in mind when he got to the rendezvous, to trade the pants off every man at the gathering and then, later, to team up with Obediah Jones. He fully expected to be successful at both.

Before he got to the top of the low, grassy ridge, Jasper could hear the noise of the revelry on the other side of the hill. He dismounted and ground tied his horses just below the top of the ridge. He knew full well that a careful man, one who wants to keep his hair or his furs or both, never skylines himself on a ridge line. Jasper's moccasins hissed in the cool, damp grass as, half running and half crawling, he reached the crest of the ridge. Darkness was rapidly falling over the camp and the black figures of the revelers flashed in and out of the flickering light of several fires. One large fire was burning in the middle of the camp.

Viewing what he considered a scene of debauchery, Jasper gave a grunt of disgust. "Wagh! Jest like they always is," he whispered to himself. "Looks like another week a teachin' them children the ways a the Lord," he muttered, as he returned to his horses.

Jasper trotted his animals into the camp and surveyed the scene with obvious distaste. The camp was filled with drunken mountain men and even drunker Indians. Indian women were being wildly pursued throughout the camp and would have been in great danger, had less rocky mountain brew been consumed earlier.

Dismounting, Jasper walked to the main fire. "Where's yer golden calf, ya filthy heathen revelers?" he hollered at the top of his lungs. Only the men nearest the fire paid any attention to him.

Nothing disturbed Jasper quite like sin, especially those sins of which he disapproved.

"Ya Philistines!" The screams and the general uproar of the camp all but drowned out Jasper's calls to repentance.

One offender rose from behind the fire. "Who is diz *mangeur de lard* wat comes among ze giants of ze mountains and speaks like ze old squaw?" the French-Canadian trapper boomed out.

Silence descended on the camp like a black cloud. The drunken men stopped in their tracks. Jasper Pughsey had been thoroughly insulted before the entire camp.

Jasper refused to believe his ears. "Pork eater," he whispered, squinting through the fire and smoke at the black outline of the figure opposite him. "Old squaw," he hissed.

Drunken pursuits were immediately forgotten and all present turned their attention on the two rough figures facing each other over the fire. Without warning, the giant Frenchman leaned across the fire and struck an unbelieving and startled Jasper Pughsey squarely in the mouth. Amid the flashing lights, Jasper heard the crunch and tasted the blood in his broken mouth. The man lunged through the fire scattering sparks and burning embers in his path and grabbed for Jasper's throat.

Outraged at the indignity of being insulted and assailed without warning, Jasper quickly stepped to one side, and the big trapper fell to the ground, tripping over Jasper's outstretched foot. In one quick movement the man was back on his feet and again lunged for Jasper. He was stopped as Jasper buried his huge fist in the giant's belly. The big man doubled over and Jasper swung again, his fist coming up squarely into the man's face. Blood gushed from the trapper's broken nose and splattered across Jasper's fist. The man slumped to his knees. Jasper swung again with all of the force he could muster, intent on driving the big man into the ground, but the wily Frenchman ducked, grabbing Jasper by his extended arm and flipping him over his head to the ground. Jasper landed on his back, the force of his fall knocking the air out of him. His head began to swim and darkness began to consume him as he fought to regain his breath. The Frenchman jumped to his feet and raised one foot above Jasper's head in an effort to stomp him while he lay helpless. Jasper saw the dirty moccasin driving toward his face. With all of the strength left in him, he seized the huge foot and rolled with it. The trapper fell backward doubling his other leg beneath him as he fell. The crack could be heard throughout the camp as the big man's leg broke beneath the weight of his falling body. In one last, agonizing effort, the trapper tried to lunge for Jasper. Jasper finished the job with a driving right to the big man's jaw. The trapper fell back groaning by the fire.

In the space of not more than two or three minutes, it was over. Jasper had whipped the giant trapper unmercifully. The Frenchman could account for every rib in his chest. His face was a swollen, bruised lump of flesh and bone, and his leg was badly broken.

"I can't tolerate bein' a natural born leader and havin' nobody recognize that fact," Jasper said. "Ta walk amongst yer feller man and havin' 'em sa stiff-necked that they don't notice ya 's more'n this child can abide. Wagh!"

Jasper looked at the rough crowd assembled around him and shouted, "Frenchy shouldn't a questioned m' judgement like 'e did. He knows my skimpy capacity fer criticism. He an' I's tesseled b'fore."

Jasper looked at the big man laying by the fire, his dirty features distorted with pain. "Who knows how ta fix a broke leg," he hollered to no one in particular.

The crowd began to break up and the mountain men began returning to their earlier, more lusty pursuits. "Ain't nobody here what gives a hoot?" he yelled.

Jasper knelt beside his huge assailant. "I'll help ya," he said roughly. "I dun the breakin', I'll do the fixin'."

Grabbing the man by his wrists, Jasper pulled him off of his badly twisted leg. The big man cried out from the pain, but attempted to stifle it from embarrassment.

"I heered 'bout ol' Hugh Glass and how he fixed his own leg once when it was broke by a grizzly. Wagh." Jasper bent down and looked in the man's eyes. "I reckon ya knows that feelin' now, don't ya?" Jasper chuckled.

The rendezvous camp lay on the northern shore of the lake near the point at which a large, cold mountain stream tumbled into the lake. The area was covered with grass and willows grew along the shoreline. Near where the river entered the lake were several large, old cottonwoods. One had been hit by lightning and its trunk was split to the ground. The camp lay about half a mile from the stand of trees. Jasper began dragging the Frenchman toward the trees.

The big, crippled trapper groaned with agony and passed out after cursing Jasper in his pain. The dead weight of the unconscious man was almost more than Jasper could pull.

Jasper Pughsey smelled the Indian before he saw him. The sight was equal to the odor.

"Ugnh!" The Indian stepped from the willows and pushed Jasper aside, nearly knocking him down.

"What the..." Jasper said with irritation.

The Indian grasped the unconscious trapper by the wrists and pulled him along as though he had no more weight than a dead sage hen. The grateful

Jasper was much relieved by even such a rude offer
of help.

"I'm sure glad he's out," Jasper mumbled.
"Them rocks and sage brush'd hurt 'im a might, I
suspects."

"Ugnh," the Indian grunted in response.

Jasper followed the Indian and his broken,
prostrate trapper in silence. When they finally
reached the stand of cottonwoods, Jasper pointed to the
lightning-struck snag and hollered above the sound
of the nearby river, "Over here."

"Ugnh." The Indian dropped the big trapper at
the foot of the tree.

"No, no...get 'im around so's I kin get 'is broke
foot up in that there crack."

The Indian responded and Jasper jammed the
foot of the broken leg into the split tree.

"Now," he said, "you get 'im by one wrist and
I'll get 'im by t'other and we'll pull like Missouri
mules 'til 'is leg is straight...understand?"

"Ugnh."

With the trapper's foot jammed fast in the split
trunk of the old tree, the two men pulled the big man
by his wrists. Jasper's stomach began to churn, the
sight almost more than he could watch. Slowly, the
crooked, swollen leg straightened out. When the leg
finally looked straight, Jasper hunched up sufficient
courage and felt it gingerly with his thumb and
forefinger, like he was about to pick up a dead snake.

"I think we sure enough did it," he said.
"Feels like it anyways. He's gonna be one sore pork
eatin' Canadian when he comes to."

The Indian watched Jasper closely, his face a
portrait of wonder and admiration. "Ugnh!" he
said, with enthusiastic approval.

"Ugnh?" Jasper mimicked, "zat all ya kin say?"

"Ugnh."

"Ain't you somethin'."

"Ugnh."

"Here, lash these sticks t' his leg and let's pull 'im back to camp."

"Ugnh."

For two weeks, the revelry continued unabated, much to Jasper's disgust. He had made his camp in a stand of tall pine not too far from the main camp's festivities where each day, far into the night, he watched the merry activities of the mountain men with mounting disdain.

Each year fewer familiar faces showed up at the gatherings and, as he watched the lawless activities of the camp, Jasper knew his lifestyle and the rendezvous were a thing of the past. The fur trade was rapidly declining, the numbers of beaver daily diminishing in the face of the trapper's onslaught. Now, it took an especially astute mountain man to accumulate enough fur, in the course of a year, to enable him to make any profit at all.

Jasper looked through his morning fire at the activities of the camp. "Well," he muttered to himself, "'bout time this child did 'is dickerin' and moved on."

Down near the shore of the lake he could see the camp of the representative of the Pacific Fur Company. For days he had watched the drunken trappers trade away their plews of fur for a few pieces of clothing and a little money.

"Fools," he muttered. "They otter celebrate, their world's comin' t' a end, awright. Wagh!"

Taking his large bundles from the cache where he had hidden them, he began loading them on his pack horses. He had too many plews and the furs were too heavy to cary down to the trader's camp in one or two loads. He didn't want any of his plunder walking off while his back was turned. The trading was going to be difficult enough as it was.

"Ugnh."

"Damnation!" Jasper jumped and turned in a crouch, his knife blade up, to confront the Indian standing a few feet behind him. The Indian did not move, but stood relaxed.

"Ya nearly skert the buckskins off'n me. Ya otterunt do that t' a feller when he's contemplatin'." Jasper relaxed and sheathed his Green River knife. He had been careless and he knew it, and that thoroughly irritated him.

"Here...he'p me load this stuff," he said irritably.

"Ugnh," the big Indian brushed Jasper to one side and began loading the animals with ease.

Jasper Pughesy was accustomed to life in the wild and its many discomforts and he was grateful for the help, but the odor that followed the Indian was almost overwhelming.

"I gotta teach this savage some clean personal habits," Jasper muttered to himself as he watched the Indian do the heavy work, "especially if 'e's gonna faller me around."

"Ya otter try washin' once in a while."

"Ugnh."

"Yew know...washin'," he said, holding one arm high in the air and scrubbin under it with his other hand. "I say, wash...ya know?"

"Ugnh."

"Sheez. Ain't chew ever got down in some water...a...a creek or somethin'?" Jasper scratched his chin. "Yew an' me's goin' down in that lake shortly," Jasper said, as he began loading the remaining plews. "Attach yer se'f t' me and yer goin' t' have t' become civilized, considerable like."

Jasper led the horses the short distance to the trader's camp, the Indian following.

"Mornin'," the trader said, emerging from his tent.

"Yep, it is," Jasper responded.

"Quite a pile of fur."

"Yep...prime."

"Uh-huh." The trader began undoing the large plews of fur as Jasper and the Indian removed them from the horses.

"I expects you'll pay plenty fer this here kind a merchandise, huh?"

The man sorted through the pelts. "Well...it aint like it was...the beaver market's off some."

"Oh, ya," Jasper responded with irritation. "Well, mine ain't, and you and me's gonna palaver some jest t' be sure the free enterprise system ain't broke down here none."

"Oh, we'll come t' some agreement. These are some of the best I've seen so far."

"Yew jest believe it," Jasper said, feeling increasingly unfriendly toward the company man. "I do like a man with faith."

"Ugnh."

"Who the devil's he?"

"Thet's...uh," Jasper scratched his head, "le'see...uh...Grunt!" he said with his finger in the air. "Yep, that's 'is name...Grunt. Ol' Grunt's ma man. Sort of a equalizer when he feels I'm in need. Does real good, too, 'e does."

Jasper patted the startled Indian on his grimy shoulder. "He ain't one ya'd want arount if yer fixin' t' trifle with me."

"I told ya we'd come to some agreement."

"Uh-huh, you did mention that," Jasper responded, as he lay the last plew of fur before the trader who was checking each pelt in minute detail. "Well, jest remember this child's a fixin' t' spend the winter in graceful circumstances an' at great expense, thanks t' your generosity."

The two men squatted over the furs dickering until Jasper felt satisfied with the deal. Only once did he bring the possibility of Grunt's uncivilized methods of persuasion into the bargaining situation, and never once did he feel the necessity of drawing his knife.

"I'm satisfied," said Jasper, standing up and stretching his cramped legs. "They's all yers."

"A fair deal, then?"

"Reckon."

"Wish you could bring me pelts like these next year."

"Like ya said, it ain't like it was. Streams that crawled with the critters jest a year 'r two ago ain't good fer nothin' but fishin' now."

"I guess times are changin', an' few of us recognize it."

"Yep, and it ain't gonna get no better neither." Jasper stared at the lake reflectively. "Maybe never. How can a body stay free when there's nothin' but

people everywhar thinkin' they need everythin'?
Sometimes I feel like the Blackfeet. I'd like t' slit the
gizzerd of the first white man I see with a wagon on
the plains a headin' fer these mountains. No good'll
come of it, I tell ya. There's got t' be a place a man
can go without bein' smoked out by some neighbor;
somewheres he can be alone, without bother. I
wouldn't lift my little finger t' help 'em. Ain't
nobody's got no business in this country 'cept wild
and free kind, be he animal or man."

"Don't make it no worse than it is," cautioned
the trader.

Gathering his reins Jasper said, "That's how it
is." Pulling his horses behind him, Jasper trudged
back to his camp, Grunt following.

A moody Jasper Pughsey spent the night in his
camp gloomily poking at his fire and thinking of his
conversation with the trader. What he had said he
knew was true, but what it meant, he didn't know.

"Reckon I otter find Obediah," he muttered.
"Him an' me's allas figgered these things out
t'geather. He's got his self a edjacation and this
child's feelin' needful right now. Wagh."

"Ugnh."

"Damnation!" Jasper nearly jumped into the
fire. "I wish you'd quit sneakin' up on me like
that."

"Ugnh."

"Lookit...if'n yew an' me's gonna get this
friendly, yer jest gonna hafta stay where I know yer
at." Jasper looked at the big Indian who had attached
himself without asking, the everpresent odor on the
early morning air. "Small wonder yer s' skinny.
You couldn't sneak up on any thing. If'n we're
stickin' togeather, you gotta be edjacated some in the

ways a civilization." Jasper got up from his place by the fire, "Come on," he said.

Reaching in his saddle bag, he brought out a large bar of hard, yellow lye soap. "Now, lookit here...you Grunt," he said, jabbing his finger at the Indian's chest. "You Grunt...me...I'm Mr. Pughsey...me...I'm boss...you injun."

"Ugnh."

"When I calls yer name...Grunt!...you come." Jasper looked at the big Indian. "Understand?"

"Ugnh."

"Yeah, well...." Jasper cleared his throat. "Now, you an' me's gonna wash," he said, holding the coarse yellow soap in the Indian's face. "Wash...you an' me," he said, pointing at the lake. "So's you smell better."

"Ugnh." The big Indian looked interested in Jasper's gyrations, but remained noncommittal.

"Come on, let's go," Jasper said, as he turned toward the lake.

The Indian watched quizzically as Jasper started for the lake, but did not move from the fire.

"Well...come on."

"Ugnh."

"Lookit here...yer supposed t' faller me."

Jasper trudged to the shore of the lake several hundred feet away from his camp and the encroaching activities of the rendezvous. He chose a point where the willows grew right at the lake's edge. By the time he stripped and gingerly hopped out to where the water was waist deep, Grunt stood near the water grinning.

"Now ain't the time fer ya t' start talkin' 'r grinnin'," Jasper said, with some irritation. "Come on."

"Ugnh," the Indian looked puzzled and apprehensive.

"Get on in here, " Jasper said, scrubbing up a lather on his chest. "It don't have t' be done often, jest oncet in a while. Wagh!"

"Ugnh." The Indian shook his head, remaining steadfast.

"Do I have t' come an' getcha?" Jasper started out of the water. "If'n yer gonna keep company with me, there's gotta be a compromise."

Jasper Pughsey's idea of a compromise was grabbing the startled Indian by the shoulders, putting his foot in the red man's belly, and rolling backwards, throwing the thrashing Grunt over his head and out into the lake. Before the big indian could get to his feet, Jasper was on him with the huge, coarse yellow bar of lye soap.

The Indian came up with his knife in his hand.

"No," said Jasper, pushing away from the angry, confused Indian. "Lookit cher..." He lathered his hands and plastered his face with the bubbly soap. Rinsing, he handed the soap to Grunt and said, "Now...you try it."

"Ugnh," Grunt responded, putting his knife away. He hesitatingly took the soap and began rubbing it on his face.

"Aggh!" Grunt dropped the soap and vigorously rubbed a stinging, lye-filled eye.

"No...no, thet ain't the way," Jasper said, splashing water in Grunt's face, further angering the Indian. "Rub water in it...like this..."

"Hey, injun! Stick it in his eye!"

Jasper turned in the water. During the cleansing melee, a crowd had gathered on the bank to watch the show with increasing hilarity.

"I ain't seen nothin' this good in a long time," someone hollered.

"How much you chargin' Jasper? I got m' squaw right cher."

"What the...? Clear on outta here. Ain't there no sucha thing as privacy no place anymore?"

"Privacy," one hollered. "Jest ask yer injun friend about privacy."

"I'm gonna clean me some whistles," said Jasper, lunging for the shore. "Where's m' pants?"

The good natured crowd began to scatter as the red faced Jasper Pughsey reached the shore with Grunt following closely behind.

"Whew," winced Jasper when he and Grunt had reached the sparse shelter of the willows, "maybe it warren't the dirt."

"More'n likely it's the company he's been keepin' of late," one of the trappers yelled amid the retreating guffaws and laughter.

"'Course, you'd never know," offered another.

Jasper grabbed his pants, but by the time he was in any condition to administer some hard lessons, the crowd was headed back to the main camp.

"I'm leavin'," Jasper said. "This ain't no place fer a body t' find the pleasures a solitude."

By night fall, the two had traveled ten miles into the mountains.

CHAPTER 8

"Well, I don't think you'd better try it," said the doctor, feeling various portions of Butch's anatomy, and asking him to stick out his tongue. "Too much walking'll just further weaken him."

The doctor stood up and said, "Give 'im more time. He's been very sick and we're lucky he's here as it is."

"But if we can't go with the camp, how'll we find our way to the Great Basin?" asked Jennifer.

"There are plenty of folks left in Nauvoo who will be coming also, and if Butch ain't ready by then, you should be able to follow our trail. Besides, 'till the boy gets his strength back, you're better off here where it's not impossible to get help, than out on the plains where you'd be helpless if things went wrong."

"When do you think he'll be fit to travel?" asked Deborah.

"Well it's only early March." The doctor scratched his balding head, "I'd give 'im several months. He's young and should come back fast. I'd say by June or July. And don't worry about getting out west. President Young will see we all make it out there. The brethren are establishing a fund, and there'll be plenty of people to help ya."

President Brigham Young had ordered those at Sugar Creek who could travel to strike camp and move west. The Saints did not know where they were going, but knew with assurance that the Lord had a place for them in the mountains to which they would be led.

By early afternoon, the camp seemed almost deserted. All that remained in the snow and cold of Sugar Creek were those who were too sick to travel or whose wagons and provisions were insufficient.

"Now, Deborah," said Mrs. Bush, "we've left ya plenty to get by on until ya can follow us later in the spring."

"Yes, ma'am."

"You'll be safe here and Butch'll be on his feet before ya know it."

"Yes, ma'am."

"Still, in all, I hate t' leave ya."

"We'll be fine," Deborah reassured the little woman. "I'm so grateful for all you've done, and please don't worry. We'll be along shortly."

Brother Bush helped his wife up onto their wagon.

"Now, don't worry none," she said. "Other's 'll be coming and there'll be lots of help."

The wagon lurched forward and moved off around the nearby bluff.

"Oh, Debbie, what're we going t' do?" asked Jennifer.

"Don't worry. Butch is mending. We've got what we need for the time being right here. Besides," Deborah said, trying to sound cheerful and reassuring, "I'd rather travel in the summer when it's warm, anyway."

***

Butch took his time hitching the horses, as Deborah walked purposefully toward him through the sparse grass of early summer.

"Butch, where are you going?" she hollered.

Sisters, he thought, they always try t' make ya feel like yer little and helpless. Inside, he knew it was going to be up to him to get himself and his two sisters out west where he could be the mountain man he was meant to be. "What do they know, anyway," he said, half aloud.

Climbing up onto the wagon seat he said, "I'm goin' back t' Montrose."

Deborah walked up and put her hand on Nail's rump. "Just what are you going back to Montrose for?"

"Well, I figger we gotta find a way t' get this wagon fixed. That ol' crutch," Butch said, jerking his thumb over his shoulder, "won't get us to the west. The weight of the wagon'll break it, sure."

"Just how 're you going to do that?"

"I dunno, maybe I can work a trade."

"Just what've you got to trade with?" Deborah asked, incredulously.

"The cow."

"The cow?"

"Yep, the cow."

"Butch, I won't let you sell her. She's all we've got."

"She'll just slow us up. Besides, she don't give enough milk t' bother."

"Butch, we need her," Deborah insisted.

"Debbie, she's almighty slow and she don't give no milk."

"Well," tears welled up in Deborah's eyes, "she was Ma's pet, ya know."

Butch slumped on the wagon seat. "I know."

"Maybe when we get t' better grass...maybe there's not enough for her here."

"Well...anyway," Butch said, trying to sound reassuring and enthusiastic, "let's ride into Montrose and look around. We could make it sort of an outing. Maybe we can find another way t' get the wagon fixed."

The crippled wagon lumbered slowly down the rutted main street of the frontier town and stopped in front of the blacksmith's barn at the end of the main street.

"You two wait here with the wagon," said Butch, as he slid from the wagon seat. "I'm going in and see if the blacksmith has a wheel he could give us."

Deborah and Jennifer watched their young brother disappear into the darkness of the large barn. He seemed perfectly well now. It had been months since the Bush's left and only occasionally did Butch seem to favor his leg.

The heat in the barn was intense and Butch's eyes stung from the smoke escaping from the open-hearth furnace. The smithy jerked a long piece of red, glowing metal from the open furnace, dipped it into a large barrel of steaming water, layed it over a huge anvil, and began hammering it with the biggest hammer Butch had ever seen. In the enclosed barn, the sharp ringing of the hammer on the anvil seemed deafening.

The smith was a huge man. He wore no shirt and perspiration ran off his dirty face and shoulders and down his back and chest.

Butch stepped closer hoping the big man would see him.

"Excuse me, sir."

The hammer kept rising and falling in a loud, clanging, oppressive cadence.

"Mister?"

"Whatcha want, boy? Can't ya see I'm busy?"

"Yessir."

The hammering stopped and the huge, sweaty giant turned toward Butch. The heavy hammer seemed like an extention of the big man's arm.

"Well?"

"Well...sir...ya see...my wagon's outside and it doesn't have a wheel..."

"Doesn't have a wheel?"

"No sir...it's broke."

"Broke?"

"Yessir. I sorta fixed it, though, so's it'd go some."

"The wheel?"

"No, sir...the wagon. What I mean is, I need a wheel for my wagon."

"What kind a wagon is it?" the man said, turning and walking to the barn door. His large frame nearly filled the double doorway.

"Come 'ere, boy."

"Yessir."

Ignoring the two girls seated on the wagon seat, the big man walked to the rear of the wagon and ran his huge hand up and down the brace.

"Who done this, boy?"

"I did."

"You did?"

"Yessir."

"Well, sir, if that's the truth, I purely admire yer efforts. How far'd ya come?"

"From Sugar Creek."

"From Sugar Creek? Is that where ya done this?"

"No sir."

"Where, then?"

"Nauvoo."

"That's what I thought. Yer one a them Mormons, ain't ya," the man said accusingly.

Butch took a deep breath and tried to look taller. "Yessir, an' I'll trade m' cow, too..."

"Not fer one a my wheels, not fer no Mormon, even if'n he is a kid. An' I don't need no half starved cow." The sweaty giant turned and disappeared into the dark barn.

"Dirty, nasty man," Jennifer whispered accusingly to her sister.

"Shhh...never mind...he'll hear you," Deborah said.

Climbing back onto the wagon seat, Butch clucked to the horses. The wagon slowly dragged its crutch out into the street, scarring the earth behind it, and moved further into the town.

"What'll we do now?" asked Deborah. "He surely wasn't very friendly, was he?"

"Nope."

"Probably, nobody will be," offered Jennifer.

"Whoa, you two," Butch said, pulling on the reins. "Let's leave the wagon here and walk along the street. Maybe we'll see somebody who'll help us."

The street was wide and lined with wood
buildings on both sides, a boardwalk in front of each.
With nowhere to go, the three Richards children left
the horses, wagon, and cow and started up the street.

"Psst...psst!"

Butch stopped in the middle of the crowded
boardwalk and looked around for the source of the
noise.

"Psst," a dirty, round face appeared at the
corner of a nearby building. "Come'ere, kid." A
grubby finger gestured under a grubby chin.

"Me?" Butch responded self-consciously.

"Yeah...you...come 'ere."

Almost in automatic response, Butch and the
girls walked over to the alley. Standing at the corner
of the building was what appeared to be a small girl
about Butch's age, dressed in dirty coveralls, with
pigtails hanging at each shoulder.

"I heard wat you was sayin'...that you needed a
wheel fer that wagon an' all, and that you was
willin' t' trade that cow."

"Yeah?" said Butch.

"Well?"

"Well, what?"

"Well, maybe my pa can help ya."

"Really?" Butch was tired and discouraged,
but this was good news.

"Yeah...we got lots a kids at our house...that cow
would sure..."

"Really?"

"Yeah."

"Well, let's get goin'." Butch grabbed the dirty
girl and pulled her toward the wagon.

"Butch, you just wait a minute, now," Deborah said. "We aren't at all sure this is what we want to do."

"That's right. It was Ma's cow, anyway," Jennifer said.

"Look, we gotta get us a wheel if we're goin' out west with the others. Do ya wanna stay in this place?"

"Well...no," the girls said, almost in unison.

"Then, there's no choice."

The girl yanked herself free from Butch's grasp. "No there ain't, and besides, what good's that cow goin' t' do ya, anyway? We got as big a need fer that cow as y'all do fer a wheel. I seen yer wagon."

"It just don't make no sense," Butch said, pleading with his sisters, "fer us to keep that cow. We need t' fix the wagon and try t' find the others. Besides, when we catch up, there's plenty of cows."

"Oh," Deborah sighed, "alright...I guess you're right."

"Do we have to?" asked Jennifer.

"I suppose we do," Deborah said, putting her arm around her smaller sister. "Let's quit arguing and get it done."

Behind the girl, the three trudged down the alley and crossed an open field filled with weeds and littered with broken wagon parts, farm implements, and assorted junk, each intent on the problem of a mutually beneficial trade: a cow for a wagon wheel that would fit. At the far end of the field stood a decrepit shack, its silvered wood sides badly in need of repair.

"Pa!" the girl hollered, "come 'ere quick. Maybe I got us a cow."

"Maybe yer Pa ain't here," Butch suggested after a short pause.

"We can always come back," Jennifer suggested, still wanting to keep the treasured family cow.

"Naw, ol' Hawky's here...drunk mor'n likely. It's almost noon." At the sound of the man's name, Deborah froze. It was a man named Hawky who had attacked her and Jennifer in the barn last winter. Grabbing a surprised Jennifer, to whom the name seemed to mean nothing, she began to back away from the house into the field. "Butch..."

"Just a minute, Debbie," said Butch.

The girl jumped up on the ramshackle porch, pushed open the broken screen door, which hung by one loose leather hinge, and disappeared into the deteriorating shack.

"Butch, please...come over here."

"Just a minute, Debbie, they've got a wheel here and..."

A small child with a dirty face appeared at the door as the girl stepped back out on the porch. "This here's one of m' brothers. I guess the others is all out somewheres. Pa's comin'."

"Is he drunk?" hollered Jennifer.

"Naw, jest snoozin', but he don't like bein' woke none."

"Whatch wan?" asked a coarse voice from inside the shack. "Go on away."

Fear began to rise up in Deborah. It was a voice she would never forget, the same voice from the terror-filled barn. He was the man who attacked her and Jennifer. "Butch..."

"Pa, I told ya, they got a cow."

The grimey, unshaven man stepped out on the creaking porch. "Where's it at?" The dirty man had an ugly, red scar that tore from his forehead across his eye and down his cheek. It looked infected and sore.

"It's over by their wagon," his daughter said.

Pulling large suspenders up over his faded, red underwear, the man stepped off the porch. He smelled of body odor and cheap, homemade whisky, and his clothes had not been washed in some time. "Whatcha want fer yer cow?"

Butch retreated to where his sisters stood and said, "We need a wheel for our wagon."

"What kind a wheel?"

"For our big wagon over yonder."

"I ain't got none."

"Yes we do, pa...a great big one out back. Common, I'll show ya."

"Shut up...I don't see no cow."

"Mister," Butch said, "if you can help me get a wheel on our wagon, I got a cow, and that's a deal."

"Oh, it is, huh?"

Realizing that the man did not recognize her or her sister, and realizing now more than ever the need for a wheel, Deborah said," She's a cow with lots of potential, if she's fed good. If you can help us we'll go get her and the wagon right now. If not, then we'll just be going. Butch..."

"Jest hold yer horses," the man said. "I ain't said I won't help ya."

"Then, will ya?" asked Butch.

"Where's this wagon and cow at?"

"Over on the street," his daughter answered.

"Let's go see."

Deborah swallowed hard. She had to get away from this big, stinking brute. So far, Jennifer did not recognize the man and probably never would, given the shock of that horrid night in the barn. "If you're going to help us, then we'll bring the wagon and the cow here."

"A' right, go get it. Seems like I might have a wheel that'll fit somewheres around here. Skat and go find it," he said to his unkempt daughter.

"Come on, Jennifer, we'll go get the wagon. The sooner we get the wheel on, the sooner we can get out of here."

The dirty man's learing gaze shifted from Deborah to Butch. "You go help 'er find that wheel and bring it around here."

Deborah turned and ran out into the field dragging her protesting sister behind. "Debbie...stop pulling me, I..."

"Jennifer, hurry up...we've got t' get that wagon fixed and get away from here as fast as we can."

"There," the man said, getting up from the side of the wagon, rubbing his back. "Looks like it came with the wagon. It's a good wheel, too. Should last ya 'till ya get where yer goin'. Where are ya goin', anyways?"

"We're goin'..."

"We lost our parents and thought we'd join our relatives over on the Missouri," Deborah interjected. She knew what the man's reaction would be if he knew anymore than that. "Come on Butch."

"Uh...ya." he responded.

"They're Mormons," the dirty little girl said, moving nearer her father.

"Mormons?" the man responded with a mixture of surprise and anger.

"Yessir," said Butch as he and the girls climbed gingerly aboard their newly repaired wagon. "And that's a mighty good Mormon cow, too, mister."

"She really is, too," responded Jennifer, "and she gives pure white Mormon milk."

Butch snapped the reins along the backs of the two horses and the wagon lurched forward with a freedom that seemed totally alien to the two horses who were used to the slow drag of Butch's wagon crutch.

"Please be good to her," Deborah yelled over her shoulder to the receding man, his daughter peering from behind him. "She was our mother's favorite, and if we could, we wouldn't leave 'er with the likes of you."

"Deborah..."

"Oh...be quiet...you don't know..."

"Hey, you three! Come back here! I want t' talk t' ya," the angry man yelled after them.

Dust billowed behind the wagon as Buck and Nails responded to Butch's urgent commands.

"Just feel this wagon," Butch cried, "we'll be back t' Sugar Creek in no time."

"We'd better," responded Deborah, "he's one of the mob that came to Nauvoo and burned our house."

"What d' ya mean...how'd you know?" Butch cried over the noise of the rumbling wagon.

"Because he, and another man, attacked me and Jennifer in the barn when everybody else was gone."

Butch caught a glimpse of the man still following them as the wagon turned down the main street to become lost in the congestion of the busy river town. "He's still after us, but he'll never catch us now."

"Butch...I feel like a dirty traitor," said Deborah, "leaving Ma's cow with that rotten man. "He was one of the mob...I know he was...he could've been the one who..."

"Deborah...let's go back and get Ma's cow," said Jennifer, wiping tears from her eyes. "It's no fair..."

"We can't go back there now," responded Butch. "Besides, a deal's a deal, and when ya get right down to it, we got a better wheel than he got a cow. She don't give no milk."

"Maybe he'll hurt 'er," Jennifer cried.

"Naw, besides, I'll bet she wanders away. He's too drunk most of the time t' know which end t' squeeze, anyway."

Deborah wiped her eyes, "We'd best keep goin'," she said, putting her arm around her sister.

"Do you think we'll ever be where we can trust people again?" asked Jennifer.

"You find 'em all over, especially when you need them," Deborah said. "Remember the old woman across the river?"

"Yes...I guess maybe you're right," her sister said.

"Don't matter now," yelled Butch over the noise of the wagon. "We're goin' west and we'll be there before ya know it."

Montrose was quickly lost in the clouds of dust that billowed behind the newly freed wagon.

CHAPTER 9

The air was sweet and clean and the only noise to fill the night was the rustle of the river lapping at the side of the canoe as it swiftly cut the water and the haunting, eerie cry of a Sandhill Crane as it flew through the echoing pines to its nest in a marshy bend of the river.

In the darkness the big river was black as ink, but beneath the canoe, it ran clean and cold. In the light one could see the big trout on the bottom almost as if looking through a glass. They hid and fed beneath the clumps of moss that waved gracefully in the current.

The water splashed and sluiced around the paddle as the canoe left the current and glided into calmer water near the shore. It made only the lightest sound as its nose slid up on the grassy bank. The single occupant slipped quietly from the canoe and pulled it up further into the grass beneath a stand of Lodge Pole Pine. The large man stood quietly sensing the forest's reaction to his intrusion. All he could hear was the wind among the pines. The slight noise of his landing had apparently disturbed nothing or no one.

Down stream and further in among the pines, a single camp fire hesitantly lit a small clearing among the trees. Quietly, the large man moved to within a few yards of the flickering circle. The fire's single attendant was bent over a heavy frying pan cooking some pork belly. The delicious aroma reached the big man's nostrils and his stomach growled so loudly, he was sure it must have been heard.

Jasper Pughsey was never more content than when he was preparing a meal of pork belly, beans, and sourdough biscuits, or when he was stringing someone along. On this particular occasion, he was doing both. Carelessly humming to himself, Jasper reached across the fire to move the coffee pot nearer the hot coals.

Suddenly, directly beneath him, the fire exploded in a burst of orange sparks and glowing splinters. The air around Jasper's head was filled with fire from the impact of the rifle ball.

"Damn your hide, Obediah Jones," Jasper hollered as he reeled backwards from the firey explosion. "You've purely blinded me!" A buckskin clad arm caught him around his neck and the knife point stuck him at the right side of his spine, just under his rib cage. Jasper froze.

"Obediah? Obediah...is 'at you?"

Obediah Jones, a giant among the mountain men pushed his intolerant victim aside and collapsed in a laughing heap at the side of the fire, "Obediah? Obediah? Is 'at you, Obediah?" he mimicked. "Obediah?" Tears streamed down his face from the intensity of his laughter.

As one might imagine, Jasper Pughsey was not appreciative of the great humor inherent in the situation which so pleased his friend.

"Oh, hesh up. Ya otterunta done that," Jasper
insisted irritably. "I didn't know fer sure it was
you. Ya coulda got yer se'f kilt."

Such advice made Obediah laugh even harder
as he got back to his feet. "Obediah?" he mimicked.

Ignoring Jasper's exasperation, Obediah Jones
wiped his eyes and reached for the coffee pot at the
edge of the fire. "Why man, with that kind of
carelessness, I don't know how you've survived so
long in the mountains. Maybe it's because you're so
ugly. Nothing dares get too near ya."

Jasper took these suggestions with obvious
discomfort and irritation. Reaching down and
dabbing a biscut in the hot grease of the frying pan,
he said, "Jest listen ta the school marm. All that
book larnin' and he's preachin' ta me about standin'
in the fire light starin' at the fire." Jasper stuffed his
mouth with the tasty sop of biscut and bacon grease.
"Oh," he grunted, his mouth filled with bread and
pork belly and smeared with the delicious grease,
"nothin' this child loves mor'n great camp cookin'
an' givin' a smart mouth know-it-all his cumup-
pance." Jasper's eyes twinkled, and Obediah Jones
felt the first twinge of alarm.

Obediah Jones was a very savvy man, but at
times, as Jasper delighted to explain, a mite slow,
especially when he was engaged in delivering a
lecture, founded on selfrighteousness, to his
mountain friends. Obediah saw the look of growing
anticipation on Jasper's face and knew he was in
trouble.

The smell of rancid camp grease, fire smoke,
and body odor overwhelmed him as a large,
incredibly dirty arm suddenly flew around his neck
and a knee shoved hard into his back throwing him

to the ground and knocking the air from his lungs. The huge Indian was astraddle his chest with a knife at his throat before Obediah knew what was happening.

Irritated at having the tables turned on him in so graceless a manner, Obediah struggled to throw the huge Indian off, but no matter how he fought, he was pinned fast.

"Oh, my, my. Jest looky there," Jasper said, his eyes twinkling in the fire light. "How have you survived the wilderness so long? Such carelessness, tich, tich," he said, clicking his tongue "Maybe it's cuz ya gotta face what'd alarm anyone with the tender sensibilities of a wild creature." Jasper's sarcasm was pure poison.

"Get this stinking heathen off me," Obediah growled as he fought to throw his assailant. A small red line began to appear on his neck around the point of the knife.

"Not s' hard, now. Mister Jones, here, ain't use t' such treatment," Jasper said to the big Indian.

Now it was Jasper's turn to lecture and he settled into the task with great earnestness. "Now, as you know, Obediah, a true borned mountain man don't never stand over an open fire in the night. Whys he might jest get hisse'f kilt purely dead by some heathen savage. Heaven knows they's jest crawlin' all over these mountains. Why, yer many friends all throughout the west would dearly miss yer appealin' ways oncet ye was gone under. Wagh! An' to have gone sa poorly, too. What an unappealin' end t' yer great saga, my, my." Jasper sniffed lowdly. "Ken ya see now, boy? Why, heaven knows this child don't want yer true edjacation to result in yer untimely demise."

"Get 'im off me," the struggling Obediah broke in. "Jasper...I"m going to skin you alive when..."

"Yer goin' t' skin me, ya say?" Jasper grinned from ear to ear. "Don't seem as how yer goin' anywheres as of this partic'lar moment. Why you do look down right harmless fer sech a large feller."

"Did you ever think," Obediah suggested, as he ceased his struggling, "that while we're doing this square dance, we might all get caught off guard? There are a lot of Blackfeet around here, and they're not known for their tender ways with white men, as you know."

"Now, Obediah, I jest plainly don't like yer sarcastic tone a voice under these here circumstances," Jasper said, feeling a mite uncomfortable; he knew Obediah was right. In the glee of the struggle he had become completely oblivious to anything but his triumph. "Now, if you'll admit, like the man I knows ya ta be, that you been rightly bested and properly edjacated, I'll be willin' t' shake yer hand," Jasper stood up blinking into the blackness surrounding the small camp.

"Oh, Jasper..." Obediah stifled a curse, "get 'im off me so we can eat and get some rest."

"That'll do jest fine," Jasper piously observed, "a right proper apology that was, too. Let 'im up Grunt."

Grunt sprang into a crouch, the sharp edge of his knife up and pointing at Obediah as he struggled to retain his dignity in getting to his feet. The Indian showed no signs of friendliness.

"'At's all right, Grunt," Jasper said, "relax, he's our friend." Jasper patted the big Indian on his shoulder and Grunt sat down near the edge of the fire, sheathing his knife, but watching Obediah closely.

"Where in the world did he come from?" Obediah asked, brushing the dirt and pine needles from his buckskins. "Where'd he come from, anyway...who is he? Just look at my neck."

"Ugnh." Grunt said, with obvious disdain for Obediah.

"What's the matter? Can't he talk?"

"Don't know. He don't never say nothin', so's I calls 'im Grunt. That's all he ever does anyways," said Jasper Pughsey. "Ol' Grunt, he jest fallers me around and approves of all my doin's. He rightly admires of all I does, and I purely respects his judgment."

"Huh, I'll just bet you do," said Obediah.

"Well...you of all people can't question the judgement of them what's survived in the wilderness," Jasper said. "Why, oncet I heard you say you wanted to become more Indian than..."

"Let's get at the pork belly and beans," Obediah impatiently broke in.

"Well, you said it," Jasper said, taking the frying pan from the fire and scraping its savory contents evenly onto three tin plates. "Somethin' about their excellent judgment, as I recollect."

The argument became lost as the three turned their attention to their plates.

In spite of the cold wind in the dark pines, Jasper had a restless night. He lay elated by his complete subjugation of Obediah Jones. What a coup. If only word could get out.

Obediah lay looking at the sparkling brilliance strewn across the black heavens. What had happened? How stupid! One can't help wondering about trusting others—especially friends. What if the word got out...."

Grunt lay away from the camp and the faint, telltale smoke of the near-dead camp fire. A knowing nose could follow smoke for miles, right to the camp, as if led by a beacon. He had little use for whites, only the grizzled old Jasper. Even to Grunt's primitive ways of thinking, the old trapper represented something solid, something that would preserve the mountains. Yet, the trapper's very presence was an intrusion that forebode change. The trappers had come to the west seeking solitude in the wilderness; seeking the inner renewal of clean air and cold water and pines and rock; seeking the challenge of the next ridge and heaving, painful lungs and throbbing temples, and sweat freezing on the skin beneath buckskins. They came to exploit for others and horde for themselves. Yet, their very presence was the prelude to the change each would have cursed. Others, equally strong but different were following.

A bond had inexplicably formed between the Indian and the old mountain man. And now this stranger had come. Another mountain man, but different. He talked too much and did not gesture with his hands as did Jasper, and his talk was too frequent, too smooth. But he was strong. In the fight at the campfire he had shown great strength. Grunt knew that had it not been for complete surprise—almost betrayal—the new mountain man would have been a dangerous, perhaps deadly, enemy.

The brilliance of the mountain night was beginning to dim when Obediah crawled from his blankets and felt the warm embers of the last night's fire with his foot.

"Whatcha doin'?" Jasper asked, from his bed back among the trees.

"Time to be moving."

"Build a small fire fer us."

"That's what I'm doing, Jasper."

"Yew think it's safe?"

"No."

"Then why ya doin' it?"

"I'm hungry."

Jasper silently appeared next to Obediah. "Me, too. There's Blackfeet here abouts, ya know?"

"I know. I'd like to reach the north fork of the Platte on the eastern slope within a few days."

"Why thata way? We could reach the Yellowstone in a day'r two and then it wouldn't be nothin' gettin' t' the Missouri, an' then easy pickin's from then on."

"I'd rather go South and then East. Too much Blackfoot activity up here and I don't want to get caught between them and the Sioux." Obediah rubbed his hands over the growing fire. "Where's that Indian?"

"Oh...he's asleep somewheres around here, I expect," Jasper said, placing the big frying pan on the fire.

"Where'd you find 'im?"

"Where'd 'e find me, ya mean." Jasper leaned back from the fire, avoiding the smoke. "Well, I got in a minor disagreement with a French trapper from up north. Ol' Grunt, he liket what he saw. I fairly kilt that big mouthed pork eater. Grunt, he helped me fix 'is leg. See'ns how I broke it, I sorta felt obliged..."

"Grunt's leg?"

"No...that pork eatin' trapper's. Wagh!"

"What are you going to do with him?"

Jasper began slicing more pork belly into the frying pan. "Do with 'im?"

"You're going to take him to Saint Louis and New Orleans with us?"

Jasper scratched his grizzled chin. "See whatcha mean. He's mighty useful, ya know." Jasper chuckled. "Remember last night? Wagh."

"Well, the point is..."

"I know what yer point is," Jasper replied irritably. "You want me t' get rid of im."

"Well, harsh as it sounds, we've always traveled alone and you know what would happen if we took 'im into Saint Louis."

"Yep...we'd have us the fixin's of a big time," Jasper said, as he stirred the sizzling strips of meat in the blackened pan. "Reckon I'm gonna hafta do somethin'," he said thoughtfully, "though I can't rightly say jest what."

"While you're getting breakfast, I'm going to have a quick look around. It's too quiet." Obediah said, getting to his feet. "Where'd you say that Indian—what's his name, Grunt—was?"

"I dunno. It ain't like him t' sleep through any noise of this kind," said Jasper, looking out into the damp, early morning dimness.

"Well, I'm going to look around. Where are the horses?"

"I only got two...a saddle horse and a pack animal."

"You mean there's no horse and saddle for me?"

"Now, don't go gettin' yerself all riled up. I had t' do some tradin' and there warn't no extra horses."

"Well, just how am I..."

"We'll work somethin' out," Jasper said, turning to the fire to avoid more discussion.

"Where are they?"

"What?"

"You know what," said the impatient Obediah, "the horses."

"Over yonder, in that little swale through the pines there," said Jasper, jabbing his thumb over his shoulder."

"I'll be back," said Obediah, as his silhouette mingled with the trees.

Jasper bent over and grabbed the hot frying pan. It hissed painfully, "Ouch...tarnation!" Jasper jumped to avoid the hot coals that scattered across his moccasins as he yanked his burned hand away from the hot pan. It was the only thing that saved him. Three blackfoot arrows hissed across the fire and into the ground immediately behind the spot where he had been crouched. Six painted Blackfoot braves emerged screaming from the trees opposite the fire running toward Jasper.

The grizzled old mountain man had survived too many years in the wilderness to die in this ignominious fashion. Quickly, he grabbed the hot pan, jammed it into the fire, scooped up coals and burning twigs and sticks, and hurled the flaming mass toward the Indians. The brilliant, flaming material scattered among the on-rushing Blackfeet, breaking the speed and coordination of their attack.

One Indian grabbed at his eyes and fell to the ground screaming in agony. Two others broke their stride in an effort to shake the coals and flaming material from their chests and pants.

Jasper turned and ran into the thick pines in the direction of Obediah and the horses. "Blackfeet! Run...Obediah...run!"

At full run Jasper entered the small swale where he had picketed the horses the night before. It was empty. His breath coming hard, he ran through the wet grass of the small meadow and into the trees, three Blackfoot braves only a few paces behind him. In the blurr of the forest, Jasper saw Obediah lunge from behind a fallen snag some fifty paces ahead of him. He felt Obediah's knife pass his head and heard the heavy thud as it hit the chest of a Blackfoot behind him. Jasper did not turn to look. His body seemed to move of its own will and not through any conscious thought process. He could hear the others closing behind him. He was going to die—he knew it for sure.

The two mountain men broke through the trees at the edge of an old cutbank where the ground fell steeply below them and lunged down the embankment, dirt and rocks scattering in the dust. The pursuing Indians emerged from the forest before Jasper and Obediah reached the bottom of the ancient embankment. Seeing their prey, the three Blackfeet screamed their sense of impending victory and hurtled down the steep embankment. Two other braves ran from the trees and slid down the slope behind them.

Jasper's lungs were about to burst. As he recovered his balance and ran into the pines at the opposite side of the dry creek bed, he quickly looked over his shoulder. "They's...five...of 'em, now," he rasped at Obediah who was lunging through the underbrush and pines a few paces ahead.

The sweat stung sharply as it ran down their faces into the open cuts where the hanging bows and brush had whipped at the two runners. They ran headlong, escape the only thought shared by the two of them. Jasper's breath was a rasp in his throat. He ignored the pain, knowing that Obediah was suffering, too, though he had hardly broken stride since the nightmare had started.

Suddenly, the two runners broke from the forest and ran into a large open, rolling prairie of knee high grass and sage brush. The next line of pine covered hills lay several miles across the open expanse.

"Jasper," Obediah rasped over his shoulder. "The Buffalo.... its only a mile or two... keep running...."

Jasper had no idea how far they had run, or how close their pursurers were. He glanced quickly over his shoulder. The nearest brave was twenty yards behind him and the next was at least fifty yards further behind. The others could not be seen. The nearest Indian had his lance raised high, struggling to get close enough to hit one of the two fleeing mountain men.

A sudden wave of nausea hit Jasper. I'm gettin' too old fer this, he thought. Dizzy...I'm gettin' dizzy. It seemed to Jasper as if his legs were running beyond his control and he thought he was gaining speed, but he kept feeling dizzy and the pounding in his ears felt as though his head would explode. He fought to keep his eyes on the center of

Obediah's head to prevent himself from losing balance.

Suddenly, Obediah seemed to leave the ground and float gracefully into the air. Jasper knew he was passing out when his own feet left the ground and he shot out into space. The cold water on his skin was a blast of ice. He could not get his balance in the swift current and his raw lungs burned within him as he fought to keep from going under the deep, boiling water of the Buffalo. The swift current carried the two exhausted men out into the river toward the opposite shore. The wild river made a sharp bend to the west and the far bank was cut deeply and strewn with drift wood and fallen pines. The two tired men struggled to hide themselves in the tangle of trees and river debris.

"Where they at?" Jasper gasped, pulling himself into shallower water behind the half-submerged logs.

Obediah coughed and spat out a mouth full of water. "Nowhere...I don't see them anywhere...do you?"

"Ya don't suppose we lost 'em, do ya?" Jasper sputtered.

The river and the opposite ledges of bank were empty.

"Only one thing's wrong with all this," said Jasper, the pounding in his head finally beginning to subside.

"What's that?" panted Obediah.

"We done lost all our possibles...all our food...our horses...our guns. Hard times, Obediah, hard times."

CHAPTER 10

It was late afternoon before Jasper Pughsey and Obediah Jones moved from behind the sodden refuse the river had piled against the deep cutbank. All day they had remained hidden watching the opposite bank for any sign of life. Their pursuers did not show themselves at the river's edge, but the two mountain men knew that cruel, sudden and final death could be lurking in the tall grass of the prairie not far from the river.

"Be dark in a spell, " said Jasper.

"Well...should we get out of here?"

"A body can't be none too careful, and I don't look forward t' another chase like the last one. I still ain't sure what happened."

"We got jumped, that's what happened."

"Wagh."

"That's what happens when you get too friendly with strange Indians."

Jasper bristled. "Jes what'd ya mean by that?"

"That Indian friend of yours...that's what I mean."

The shivering Jasper squinted at his cold and wet friend, "So that's how yer stick floats, is it? Honest t' goodness, I sometimes fear fer ya. After all I done t' learn ya the ways of the mountains. Yer still a no account pork eater."

"What d' ya mean by that?" Obediah shot back.

"Yew don't know poor bull from fat cow, that's what I mean by that. Grunt weren't no Blackfoot."

"Well, what was he? He was an Indian, and about as savage as they come."

"I dunno what 'e was...too dirty to tell, but he sure 'n tarnation wasn't no Blackfoot, sure as my rifle has hindsights."

"Well, where was he when we needed him?"

"Yew can call him what ya like, but smart's what 'e is. He was plumb gone when the trouble started. Fer all I know he was gone before we was asleep."

"I suppose. I have to get moving or I'll never move again."

"Me, too. I can't barely feel nothin' from my neck down."

"I think its dark enough that if we stay in the river and let the current carry us down stream, we won't be seen."

"Sounds possible, but the river's goin' the wrong direction."

"Come on...let's go."

Quietly, they slipped from behind the log jam toward the main current of the river and let its force carry them off down stream, two bobbing pieces of refuse in the wild river.

The two mountain men lay in the tall grass at the side of the river, their sodden buckskins clingling icily to their cold, shivering bodies. The night air was crisp with chill.

"How far down stream ya figger we come?" asked Jasper.

"A mile or two, I'd guess. No more."

"Sure was a bumpy ride."

"It was...I'm nearly frozen to death."

"Reckon we otta build us a small fire?"

"Too chancy," said Obediah. "Let's start moving and see how far we can get. Seems like this is pretty crowded country. Maybe we can find some of your red brothers and relieve them of their horses before they relieve you of what little hair you've got left."

"It ain't me they'll scalp," Jasper said, getting to his feet. "I ain't got enough left t' bother with. It's your lovely curls they'll admire."

Obediah and Jasper began trotting in an easterly direction away from the river that had saved their lives.

"Let's see how far we can go before we have to stop," Obediah suggested. "Our bodies should warm with this movement."

"Well...I jest got t' tell ya, I'm about plumb run out. My ol' legs got bigger knots in 'em than most a these pines."

Jasper suddenly stopped, jabbing his elbow into his companion's chest. "Did ya get a whiff a that?"

Obediah sniffed the night air. "Smoke."

"Yep...faint, though."

"Where's it coming from?"

"Off ta the right...only sort of straight ahead, I'd guess," Jasper said. "It must be a ways off...sorta comes an' goes."

"Come on, but be careful."

The two men moved swiftly on owls wings through the dense forest, their moccasins making little noise on the thick forest floor. The trees thinned as the ground became rocky and began to rise steeply to a ridge line.

"I've lost it," said Obediah.

Jasper sniffed. "Me, too, but maybe if we get up in those rocks we can see what's on the other side of this hill."

"Whoever it is has got t' be around here some place."

Jasper and Obediah moved into the confusion of the rocky outcropping at the base of the ridge. Nearing the top of the talus they slid to their stomachs and crawled to the broken ridge line.

"Fresh smoke, sure as my stick floats," whispered Jasper.

"Over there...on the other side of the rock slide."

Before them lay a talus of loose rocks that had sluffed away from the broken outcroppings at the top of the ridge. The rocky mass fell away to the south and became lost in the thick forest below. Across the rough talus, a camp fire winked at them hesitantly.

"How far ya figger?" asked Jasper.

"Half a mile...maybe more."

"Injuns?"

"Maybe...at least I'd guess so."

"Whoever it is, I hope they've got horses."

"Well, were not going to find out laying here talking about it."

"Otterunt we t' have a plan?" asked Jasper.

"Seems like a passable idea," responded Obediah.

"Well?"

"Well, what?"

"What's our plan?"

Obediah looked at his old friend lying beside
him in the darkness. "What ever we do, let's do it
right this time. That's a plan."

"Well," said the exasperated Jasper Pughsey,
"seems like that goes without sayin'."

"It always does, but somehow things never
seem to go right." Obediah shifted position on the
hard ground. "Let's just be direct about the whole
thing. We'll scout the camp and if it's trappers or
whites, we'll palaver. "

"What if'n it injuns?"

"Well...let's locate their horses first, then see if
we can make off with some possibles, grab two or
three horses and light out fast. We know this country
as well as they do, so we can head south and cover as
much territory as possible. If we scatter the rest of
their horses, we'll be far gone before they get
organized...at least as organized as those Indians
are likely to get. What do you think?"

"Passable."

"You got a better idea?"

"Nope."

"That's what I thought. Let's go."

Cautiously, the two conspirators ventured out
onto the rock slide.

"This stuff is looser than it looks," whispered
Obediah.

Jasper grunted in agreement. "One bad move
an' it's a free ride t' the bottom. "

"True...broken legs and all."

The weight of the two men made the rock slide
move slightly with each step and a few loose rocks
tumbled down the slide with an annoying clatter.

"This isn't what I'd call quiet."

"Nope."

The two men stopped and crouched in the middle of the slide to listen for any possible hostile reaction to their progress.

"Yew think they heard us?" asked Jasper.

"I don't know. This is no place to get caught."

The two men remained quiet for some time and, sensing no reaction to their presence, began climbing across the remainder of the broad, steep talus.

"A few more yards and we'll be on solid ground."

"When we get there," whispered Jasper, "let's lie low and let the air clear."

"Good idea...the way sound travels in these mountains, they had to hear us."

"Maybe they figgered it was a deer or some varmint."

"Let's hope so."

Seconds seemed like hours before the two finally reached solid ground. Finding a hiding place among the brush of the hillside, each strained to hear any sounds that would indicate their quarry had heard their slow and noisy progress across the rock slide.

"Seems quiet enough."

"Yep...kind a worrisome, I'd say."

"Maybe too quiet."

"Still...their camp's a ways off."

"I know, but ya can't be too cautious."

Moving as quietly as each knew how, Jasper and Obediah approached the small circle of flickering light cast by the dying fire. A horse blew and stomped

"Hear that?" asked Obediah.

"Yeah, the horses are on the other side of the camp."

"See anything?"

Jasper squinted into the darkness trying to decipher the shapes and shadows that danced at the edge of the dying firelight. "Looks like maybe four or so," he whispered.

"Yeah...and maybe one or two more out here somewhere keeping guard," whispered Obediah.

"What d' you make 'em out t' be?"

"Shoshoni, from the looks of things, but I don't think it's a war party.

"Look...up through there...in that pine...meat, maybe."

"It's the quarters of a deer, I'd guess.

"Yep, a huntin' party, fer sure," said Jasper.

"I don't think they've even posted a guard."

"Seems unlikely...but I'd guess yer right."

"Did you hear that?" Obediah whispered.

"What?"

Obediah pointed off to their right. "It came from over there," he whispered.

"A picket?"

"I don't think so. Something's..."

A dark figure emerged from under one of the blankets on the opposite side of the fire and peered off away from the camp in the direction of the noise in the underbrush.

"Looks like he heard it, too," whispered Jasper.

The figure melted with the shadows and silently moved off to investigate.

Obediah touched Jasper's elbow. "Come on, let's go around this way, he said, pointing to his left. "I want to be near the horses in case some action starts."

"My thinkin' exactly," whispered Jasper.

The horses stomped nervously as the two mountain men approached.

"They've got our scent," said Obediah.

"Ugh-ugh," said Jasper, "the wind's the wrong direction. Somethin' else is spookin' 'em."

The horses were tied to a long rope stretched between two large pine trees. The two mountain men quietly began untying the first two horses they came upon, gently rubbing the animals' noses to keep them calm.

Obediah began backing his horse away from the others as Jasper struggled in the dark with the knot securing his horse to the tethering rope.

"Easy, boy," whispered Obediah.

"Tarnation!" hollered Jasper as his horse began to rear wildly.

In the melee that erupted, both Jasper's and Obediah's horse began rearing in an effort to break loose as an Indian yelling and screeching broke into the camp at full run, a huge grizzly bear close behind. The bear began bawling loudly and tearing at any object within the dim circle of firelight. The Indians, startled from their unsuspecting sleep, began running wildly in every direction in an attempt to avoid the angry bear's charges.

"Watch yer se'f, Obediah," hollered Jasper, as two frantic Indians ran toward the horses.

"I'll get 'em. Hang on to these two and untie the rest of the horses so they'll scatter."

While Jasper hurriedly busied himself with the wildly rearing horses, the unsuspecting Indians ran face first into a large dead pine branch which Obediah swung before they saw it coming. Both fell like rocks from the blow.

With the camp occupants scattered, the bear caught the scent of both the milling, frightened horses and the fresh meat hanging in the branches of the nearby pine tree.

Taking advantage of the bear's momentary confusion and the almost total rout of the Indians, Obediah slipped into the camp searching for any object that would enhance their chances of survival until they could find the necessary supplies they desperately needed.

"Hurry, Obediah" Jasper hissed.

"I'm coming," Obediah hollered, as he struggled to mount one of the skittish horses.

Frightened by the scent of the rampaging bear and the total confusion in the camp, the two horses bolted into the forest oblivious to the trees and brush about them.

As the two men got control of their mounts and headed in a southerly direction away from the Indian camp, Jasper said with some pride," I allas did say that surprise'd whip and Indian every time Never in my borned days did I see such out manuverin' as we jest done."

"Jasper, I think the bear had something to do with it," Obediah hollered.

"What'd ya find in that camp?" Jasper asked, as the two riders slowed their excited horses to a fast trot.

"I managed to grab a bullthrower...a Hawkin from the looks of it."

"Obediah...I allas did say you was the ha'r of the b'ar," Jasper said, delighted with the additional luck.

"Only one thing wrong, though."

"What's that?"

"No powder and no galena."

The two men road in silence for several minutes. The gentle down-hill slope made the going easy and the forest became less dense, periodically opening into broad meadows divided by small streams of water. The black sky was beginning to fade with early morning light.

"Hold on, Obediah," said Jasper, reigning in his nervous horse.

"What's the matter," asked Obediah, quickly surveying the dim forest.

"Nothin...'cept I been thinkin'. Since yer s' all fired bent on gettin' t' the Platte, let's cross the Snake and head fer Pierre's Hole. I'll bet my buckskins we'll find somebody down there ta palaver with and stock up on possibles."

"That's kind of what I had in mind."

"Good," said Jasper. "When we get our possibles together, we can head east below the three spiky Tetons t' Jackson Hole, then on over t' Union Pass and down t' the North Platte. Otterunt take us more'n a couple of weeks, takin' it easy like."

Morning came to Pierre's Hole quite unlike anything seen anywhere else in the world. To Jasper Pughsey, the Hole was one of the most beautiful places in the west. It lay below the west slopes of the Grand Tetons in a heavily timbered area that filtered the morning light into a misty softness that made the cottonwoods and aspen seem to glow in a soft haze.

The smoke from the fire drifted up through the dwarf oak surrounding the camp and lent an air of

mystery that would linger until the sun rose above
the ragged Teton peaks and spilled a glimmering
brilliance over the aspen shimmering silently in the
late morning breeze. The air was crisp, clean, and
smelled lightly of wood smoke.

"I'd say we done right well," said Jasper,
straightening up from the camp fire.

Pork belly and eggs sizzled in a blackened
kettle and made the men's mouths water as they
packed their newly acquired belongings and
prepared for the journey that lay ahead.

"I'd say so," grunted Obediah, as he lifted a
rack to the back of a dozing pack horse won in a high
stakes game the day before. "You were lucky to get
your hands on that Hawkin."

"Yep...I still can't believe it. Finest bull
thrower a man could get 'is hands on an' it's all
mine."

"True enough. And all of the rest of this
plunder should last us until we reach the Missouri
and Fort Atkinson. I don't think we'll even need to
stop at Fort Laramie, unless we decide we want to."

Jasper snickered, "I'll never ferget the look on
that Injun's face when I opened m' hand in that
game and there warn't no bone t' be found. He
thought his medicine was sure enough powerful not to
lose his horses and that Hawkin after 'e done all that
groanin' and dancin'."

A couple of well spent days, I'd say," said
Obediah. "We've got flour and beans, lead and
powder. Can't ask for more."

"Yep...these is shinin' times." Jasper sighed
and looked off into the timber. "This child purely
misses the real rendezvous we used t' have. A camp
like this'n ain't nothin'. Neither was the one down

on Bear Lake a while back. Ain't had what y'd call a
real one fer nearly ten years, now."

"Yep," agreed Obediah, "those times almost
seem lost to us now."

"Them was shinin' times warn't they,
Obediah?"

"Yes," said Obediah, scratching an itch,
"things are changing. Fewer and fewer beaver,
most of the mountain men seem to have gone under
or drifted off, and even the Indians seem different,
somehow." Obediah pulled a cinch and turned back
to the fire. "Let's eat," he said, trying to break the
increasingly melancholy mood.

The pork belly and eggs tumbled onto the plates
in a steaming, aromatic pile. The smell of the food,
of pine and oak, of smoke mixed with other camp
smells, gave a zest to life, but added further to
Jasper's moodiness.

"How long you figger it'll take us t' get to the
North Fork of the Platte?"

Obediah took another steaming spoonful of
eggs and pork belly. "Oh...a day or two to the Wind
River, then we should cut down to the Popo Agie;
spend a day or two there, depending on the sign; then
down to the Sweet Water and follow it on over to the
North Fork. It's rugged country, but we're in no
hurry. Once we get to the Platte, it's clear sailing.
We'll be in Saint Louis before you know it. Cheer up,
partner. Good times are staring us right in the
face."

"What we gonna do fer money?"

Scraping his plate clean, Obediah returned to
packing the horses. "I don't know...we'll make out
somehow...we always have, haven't we?" Let's get
moving."

Highly prizing their scalps, the two mountain men exercised prudence in their travels, avoiding all contact with Indians. And with great anticipation of what Jasper began calling their big rendezvous in Saint Louis and New Orleans, the two made slow but determined progress to the upper reaches of the Platte River. Once on the shores of the gentle, broad river, they made excellent time toward their much anticipated, dissolute pleasures on the Mississippi. The Platte River Valley escorted them from their familiar, beloved mountains far out onto the great American prairie.

CHAPTER 11

The two men crouched in the undergrowth, well back in the blackness of the trees. To anyone but the most trailwise, there was nothing in the trees surrounding the camp but thick brush.

"I tell ya, Obediah, we don't want nothin' ta do with 'em. They's pure p'ison," Jasper Pughsey whispered urgently.

Obediah Jones watched the flickering camp and the two girls moving about in the orange glow of the fire.

"You know dadburned well they's Injuns about," Jasper hissed in exasperation. "You mess around here an' we'll all get our hair lifted, sure." Jasper's legs were beginning to ache and he wanted to get moving. "An' wat fer," he continued, "a bunch a kids what'll never survive out here, anyways. Wagh!"

"Well...I don't know what they're doing out here, Jasper, but you know as well as I do, they're in trouble," Obediah whispered. "All we did yesterday was cut Injun sign. There are war parties all over the place. If these kids stumble onto them, it'll be the end of 'em." Obediah shifted his position slightly to ease his cramped legs.

"You know what they'll do to those two girls. Even you can't ignore that," Obediah said, glancing

at the dark form of his old friend. "Now, hush up. If
they don't hear us, Injuns might," Obediah hissed.
"Let's just sit here a minute and see what they're up
to, if they look like they know how to handle
themselves."

Deborah was so tired she could have fallen in
her tracks. She had placed a large pan full of water
next to the fire. "We've got to clean these things up so
we can move at first light," she said.

Her sister sat staring into the fire, wrapped
snuggly in a big blanket. "Oh, I wish Ma and Pa
were here." Every time Jennifer mentioned her Ma
and Pa, she felt hysterical. She had never felt so
alone in her life.

"Deborah, I'm so scared. We don't have any
idea where we are or how to find the Great Basin.
What are we going to do?" She had not felt such
despair since they had left Nauvoo. "Debbie, it's
getting cold. It's almost September. What if it
snows?"

The full moon made the night a world of silver
and black contrasts. Though they were still far from
the mountains, the prairie wind had a chill to it. In
the high passes of the Rocky Mountains, fresh snow
was beginning to accumulate in shaded areas.

"All we can do is keep on, Jennifer," Deborah
responded. "What alternatives do we have?" She
leaned over the fire and moved a large pot of boiling
water to one side, waving one hand in front of her
face to keep the smoke from her eyes. "The saints
went this way. You can tell many wagons passed
through here earlier this summer. Brother Bush said

to follow the Platte River 'til it forked, and then to stay with the North Fork until we reached Fort John." Deborah stacked dirty cooking utensils on the ground near the pot of hot water. "Jennifer, don't just sit there, help me with these things."

Jennifer got up from her place near the fire, dropping her blanket over the tongue of the wagon. The fire was built just a few feet from the end of the tongue at the left of the wagon. The rear of the wagon protruded out into the silver-blotched blackness.

"Jennifer, please don't be afraid," Deborah pleaded. "We left the river fork a week ago and since yesterday we haven't been able to see the South Fork." Deborah poured half of the hot, steaming water into a second large kettle. "I'll wash; you dry," she said. Using a large bar of rough, yellow soap her Ma had made, she began lathering and rinsing each dish. "Fort John can't be more than two weeks away." She tried to sound cheery and hopeful, but inside she knew that if bad weather hit them, they would be in trouble. With a good storm, the prairie could turn into a sea of mud and the horses' hooves would sink deep, making the weight of the big wagon too much for them to pull. The horses looked none too good as it was.. There was plenty of forage on the plains, each day they walked in a sea of grass, but the further west they got, the poorer the forage was becoming. And, on top of everything, yesterday the impatient Nails had thrown a shoe. Butch had replaced it, but....

"Where's Butch?" asked Deborah, suddenly missing her small brother.

"He said he was going to check the horses," Jennifer said, straightening up and peering into the darkness. "I think he's worried about Nail's foot," she said, returning to her work. "He's probably looking around. He's become quite a man."

"I wish he wouldn't be quite so all-fired independent," Deborah said, with some irritation. "After dark he should stay with us in camp."

"He'll be all right." Jennifer walked to the wagon and stacked the dishes in their place. "He's a man now, you know." She felt choked. "He has t' be now Pa's gone."

"I know, but he's still my little brother. I guess he always will be," Deborah said, glancing out into the silver night.

Deborah's worries continued to increase. Their late start because of Butch's leg being slow to heal, the late season to be starting across the plains, and then, two days ago, she had seen a lone Indian sitting on his horse atop a barren bluff between the two Plattes. He must have been nearly a mile away, but she was sure it was an Indian. She could not make out his features at such a distance, but he looked nude and held a long staff with what looked like feathers at the top of it. She was sure he had been watching them, but she did not know for how long. Then the wagon had gone down into a large gully. When it emerged on the other side, the Indian was gone. Deborah had told no one. Jennifer was scared as it was, and Butch would have immediately felt compelled to "check it out," as he always put it. Deborah didn't like the night; it threatened her.

Butch lay in the deep grass not far from where the hobbled horses were grazing on the rich gama grass at the edge of the trees. He was staring at several dimly-seen footprints in the soft earth. The boy had literally stumbled on them by accident. He had gone to check on the horses, especially Nail's hoof, and decided to circle the camp just to check things out. His foot had caught in the branches of a small, fallen tree and he had pitched face forward into the soft, damp earth. There, at the end of his nose in a bright patch of moon light, were the footprints. When Butch recognized what they were, he froze. The prints were fresh. The edges were sharp and no loose dirt had sluffed into them. Whoever had made them was being extremely cautious. No other foot prints could be seen except right at this spot.

The intruders had stepped over the fallen snag in an effort to remain silent in their approach to the camp. Stepping on the tree might have caused a twig to snap or the dry branches to rustle against the ground.

Pa had once told him that if a good tracker could study a man's track, he could see the man's face in it; follow him for an hour and he would know in some detail the kind of person he was following. The only thing Butch could tell was that there was more than one individual. He saw five indentations around the fallen sapling.

For the first time, the small boy felt like a real mountain man. He lay in the damp, sweet-smelling grass with real footprints before him and unknown enemies between him and his camp. He was scared, but he felt genuine excitement.

Butch was sure they were Indians. "Savages," he whispered under his breath. Then he remembered the Kentucky Long back in the wagon. He clenched his grubby fists, his forehead on the ground, "Why didn't I bring th' rifle." He felt amateurish and stupid. If he were caught by the savages this way, he would never forgive himself. What would Pa think,

and his sisters. He had to get back to the wagon
without being seen.

Butch got up slowly, cautious that he not make
any sudden, out-of-the-place movement or sound,
and melted with the silver and black patches among
the trees. Luckily, a light breeze was blowing and
the leaves flickered and moved in the lonely moon
light helping to cover any movement. The boy
moved through the trees as quietly as a ten-year-old
boy can in the dark and in a hurry, his clumsy boots
hissing in the deep, damp grass. He stayed within
the outer edge of the trees and circled the camp to the
rear of the wagon. Untying the rear flap, he climbed
into the dark interior. Butch found the long rifle
where he carefully kept it concealed and crawled to
the front flap, above the wagon tongue. There he
would wait and catch their assailants unaware
should they be foolish enough to attack his camp.

The newly self-aware mountain man lay
patiently in the wagon watching his two sisters busy
themselves with the dishes and getting things ready
to repack for tomorrow's march. Twice he heard
them mention his name and several times the girls
looked out into the night. If they'd just stay put and
not go lookin' for me, he thought, things'll be all
right. Butch felt confident that he now held the upper
hand. Whoever was out there didn't stand a chance.

Time passed, and Butch lay in the wagon
staring at the flickering fire. He was very tired and
had worked hard. They had made twelve miles that
day and he had walked all of it beside the wagon.
The fire had a mesmerizing effect and his eyes grew
heavy. Each time he dozed, Butch shook his head
with renewed determination to stay awake.

Once Jennifer had come and replaced some cooking equipment in the wagon, but she failed to see her stealthy young protector at his post in the front of the wagon. He simply looked like another bundle. Butch was asleep, the muzzle of the long rifle barely protruding from beneath the wagon's cover.

"Somethin's missin'," Jasper murmured after watching the camp in cramped discomfort.

"Yes...there's got to be three of them." Obediah slowly stood up beside a large tree, his form blending with the silhouette of brush and trees. It felt good to stretch his cramped legs and let the blood return to his aching muscles.

"From the looks a them tracks back by their tethered horses, its a young'n," Jasper deduced, joining Obediah at the side of the tree. "I'd make 'im t' be mebby nine or ten, whatchew think?"

The two men spoke in low, hushed tones.

"I'm wondering where he is."

"Uh-huh."

"Looks like his sisters have missed 'im, too."

"Yep. Say, ya don't suppose th' little rascal spotted us, do ya?" The thought of being caught by a mere boy was thoroughly distracting to Jasper.

"What would that do for your reputation," Obediah chuckled. A light breeze played in the grass and trees, silver leaves flickered in the moonlight.

"'t ain't funny," Jasper grouchily concluded.

"Well, instead of us sitting here like a couple of scared coyotes, let's just go in and get acquainted," Obediah whispered. "If the boy's around, he'll show up when we do."

"Yeah, but what if'n he's got a gun and lacks a mite in experience and judgment. He probably ain't never heered a our reputation."

"You figure that would change things, do ya?"

In the darkness, Jasper couldn't see the grin splitting Obediah's face.

"Well...it sure has elsewheres, in more experienced circles," the old trapper responded.

Obediah cupped his hands to his mouth.

Jasper grabbed him by the arm. "Whatcha doin'?" he hissed in exasperation.

"I'm going in and see what those kids are doing out here. If they're not in trouble now, they aren't far from it. The worst kind of trouble is not knowing when you're in it, and it looks like that's the kind they've got," Obediah insisted.

Obediah pulled his arm free and cupped his hands to his mouth. "Halloo, the camp!"

Jasper's form melted into the dark montage of trees and brush that surrounded the two men.

"Oh!" Jennifer jumped straight in the air.

"Oh, dear," Deborah said.

Both girls ran to the opposite side of the fire in an effort to use it as some sort of barrier between them and the unexpected voice. They peered through the fire and smoke into the darkness beyond.

"Who could it be?"

"I don't know, but we've got to stay calm and look like we can protect ourselves."

"How do we do that?"

"Halloo, the fire! May I join you?"

"What are we going to do?" Jennifer whispered urgently.

Neither girl could see anything but blackness beyond the circle of firelight. Both had repeatedly stared into the fire as they cleaned their cooking utensils and their eyes were unadjusted to the dark.

The big man appeared at the edge of the fire light. He seemed to assemble from the darkness around him like some sort of apparition. He was tall and dressed in yellow buckskins with fringe hanging the full length of his sleeves and down the sides of his pants. He looked clean and wore no beard. Under his arm was a rifle sheathed in a long, fringed buckskin scabbard. He wore moccasins and moved like a shadow.

"May I warm myself at your fire? The night is chilly," he said, moving nearer to the fire. He spoke with the refinement of a well educated man.

Both girls were frozen between fear and fascination.

The big man smiled and said, "May I have a cup of coffee?"

"We don't drink it," Jennifer blurted. "Oh," she said, covering her mouth with her hand, startled by the sound of her own voice.

"I'm sorry," Obediah Jones said. "May I sit down?" He gestured to a large rock near the fire.

The girls were standing between the fire and the wagon, with their backs to the wagon where Butch guarded them in his sleep. The big man seated himself at the side of the fire where he could watch the girls and the wagon without looking through the fire. In the wilderness, staring at a fire amounts to the same thing as being blind. A man is helpless without his night vision.

"I'm sorry, please do sit down," Deborah said, too late. She gathered control of herself. "We've just finished eating, but I can offer you some baking powder biscuits and smoked ham."

"I don't want to take what little you may have, but I am hungry."

"We have plenty," Deborah lied."

"Deborah!" Jennifer said, pleadingly.

"We have plenty," Deborah insisted, and turned toward the wagon.

Obediah watched her carefully as she stepped up on a large wheel spoke and reached into the wagon. A lid clattered sharply on the floor of the wagon, and Deborah returned to the fire with a large, black kettle containing a small piece of smoked ham wrapped in cheesecloth. She carried several hard biscuits in her other hand.

The clatter of the kettle lid jarred Butch from his sleep. He jumped so hard at the sound, he was sure someone had heard him. Remembering his mission, he peered beneath the wagon cover. The big mountain man sat only a few feet from the end of Butch's long rifle talking quietly with Deborah as she fixed his scanty meal. Slowly the boy raised the big gun to his cheek and shoulder.

"My name's Obediah Jones," he heard the big man say.

Deborah kept crossing back and forth between him and the man at the fire as she made his sandwiches of biscuits and meat and took them to him.

"I'm sorry we have nothing warm to give you to drink."

What's she bein' sorry to him for, Butch thought, that's the last of our grub. Now Jennifer was between him and the man. If th' girls'd just get outta th' way, he thought. How'm I gonna do this without lookin' funny...he's a real mountain man...and dangerous, probably. Butch's mind worked quickly.

"I'm Deborah Richards, and this is..."

"I'm Jennifer," Jennifer broke in, "and..."

"An' I'm Butch...you'd better stick 'em up." His voice was a bit too shrill and Butch began to feel silly.

The big rifle protruded dangerously from beneath the wagon cover, pointing directly at Obediah's chest. Obediah could not see who was on the other end, but the voice belonged to what sounded like a frightened boy.

At the unexpected sound of Butch's voice, both girls ran to the other side of the fire.

"Stay outta the way," Butch hollered at his startled sisters. "You heard me, mister, get'em up."

Obediah Jones set his food on the rock beside him and got slowly to his feet.

Deborah started to protest her brother's hasty action, but Obediah motioned her silent. "Looks kind of like you've got me." He didn't want a frightened boy pulling the trigger on that cannon from confusion or fright. "Why don't you come out of the wagon?" Obediah saw a movement on the right side of the wagon, out of the girl's line of vision. It was Jasper Pughsey.

When Obediah had hollered to the camp and began his haulting progression to the girl's fire, Jasper had circled the camp and come up behind the wagon. He had moved silently through the deep prairie grass on the dark side of the wagon. Deborah had dropped the kettle lid just as he had reached the big right, front wheel. He thought she might have caught a glimpse of him as he ducked under the wagon box, opposite her, but apparently she hadn't. He was again moving carefully to the front of the big wagon box when he saw the long rifle barrel slide out from under the wagon's cover.

So that's where 'e was. Jasper smiled to himself at the sound of the boy's nervous voice. The little feller's skeered. Obediah's a cool customer, though, Jasper thought, he won't do nothin' foolhardy...fer a minute, anyways.

Directly beneath the barrel of Butch's gun, across the wagon tongue lay Jennifer's blanket where she had dropped it when she went to help Deborah with the dishes.

"I'll get outta the wagon when I'm good and ready," Butch was saying. He wanted very much to get out of the cramped wagon, but he couldn't figure out how to do it without taking the gun off of this obviously dangerous intruder. He was cramped and tense and his muscles ached.

Deborah raised her hand to her mouth in surprise, "Oh!"

Jasper quickly stepped in front of the wagon, and in one swift movement swept up the blanket, threw it over the rifle barrel, and pulled down hard.

Butch's finger was stuck in the trigger guard as the big gun flew from the side of his face.

The explosion from the muzzle of the big rifle was deafening, and simultaneously the campfire exploded with the impact of the gun's discharge. Sparks, embers, and hot pieces of burning wood flew in every direction in a wild, orange spray.

"Yeow!" Butch flew from the front of the wagon behind his caught finger. He plowed into the ground at the moccasined feet of the towering Jasper Pughsey.

"Dirty bugger! Dirty Bugger!" Butch hollered, springing to his feet, his finger throbbing, and his pride crushed at being so handily disposed of.

Jennifer stood with her hands over her mouth too shocked by the rapid action before her to utter a sound.

"Butch, Ma'd beat you good if she heard that," Deborah yelled.

"That was our last charge," Butch hollered, stopping short with the realization of what he had just said.

The single report of a rifle shot reverberated dimly over the plains from somewhere off to the east. Eight painted Blackfoot warriors rose from their fire and looked into the night in the direction of the faint, but unmistakable sound.

CHAPTER 12

"Well now, you appear t' be in a real fix, don't ya?" Jasper looked down his nose with great disdain at the defeated boy at his feet. "No powder fer yer thunder stick, no food, an' I'd say poor prospects fer a very bright future."

Butch sat down on the wagon tongue and buried his face in his hands. "Oh, Geez...." His despair and embarrassment knew no bounds. Even worse, his finger throbbed and he longed for his home in Nauvoo where he could protect his emerging manhood by bawling alone in his room unseen and unheard. His own room—a place of many refuges.

"You two girls sit down and tell us what this is all about," said Obediah Jones.

"Oh, Mr. Jones," said Deborah, sitting by the fire, "we're on our way to the Great Basin to join our people."

"The Great Basin?" interrupted Jasper Pughsey.

"Yes...and others have gone on ahead of us, months ago. And I'm sure others are following, but they haven't caught up."

Jasper grunted with disgust. "So you young pork eaters are out here all alone?"

"Yes sir."

"You got any idea of where yer at and what could happen t'ya...and what time a year it's gettin't' be? Wagh!"

Jennifer collapsed in a sobbing heap next to Butch.

"Well...in all my borned days I ain't never seen nothin' sa dumb. Where's yer folks, anyways? And who's yer people?"

Deborah attempted to continue, but her voice filled with emotion.

"Jasper, it won't do if they're all upset and crying," Obediah interjected. "Let them talk."

"Our folks are dead," Jennifer wailed, "and we were driven out to Sugar Creek and..."

The talk began to spill freely from all three.

"We're Mormons," said Jennifer, "and..."

"And we can take care of ourselves," said Butch. "We don't need any of your..."

"Oh, ya don't, huh?" said Jasper, interrupting the teary tumult.

"No...and..."

"We're members of the Church of Jesus..."

"A bunch a religious pork eaters out t' get themselves kilt fer some no account cause and t' ruin the peace of the wilderness in the..."

"Now, hold on...everybody! Just hold on," hollered Obediah Jones, looking into the darkness surrounding the camp. "All of this arguing won't save you or us or the 'peace of the wilderness' if we don't take it easy and get things straight."

"Yeah, I know that much," Butch said, defiantly.

Jasper screwed up his wrinkled old face and leered down at Butch. "Oh, ya do, do ya...well let me..."

Obediah put a calm hand on his old and excitable friend's shoulder. "I've heard of your people. You're followers of Joseph Smith, aren't you?"

"The Prophet Joseph Smith," corrected Butch.

"Now lookie here, young'n..." said Jasper.

"He's right, Jasper, the Prophet Joseph Smith. To them that's what the man is...was...is..."

"They finally drove us out of our homes...our city..." Deborah began to sob, her heart filled with the apparent futility of their situation.

"Where's this Smith feller now?" asked Jasper.

"He's dead," said Jennifer, wiping her red, swollen eyes.

"And Brother Brigham's taking everyone out to the Great Basin where no one will want to bother us anymore," Said Deborah.

"Well, if you ever seen the place, you'd know that t' be the honest truth," said Jasper. "Nobody's gonna want ta bother ya there. Wagh!"

Deborah gave a big sigh and stood up. "Well, that's how it is, and that's why we're here and no one is going to stop us," she said. "We just have no alternative."

"Where's this Brother Brigham feller?" Jasper began.

"Well...no one wants to stop you," said Obediah.

"Oh, course not...this place is jest crawlin' with Injuns. We've cut sign all day, and yer tellin' these pork eatin' kids no one wants t' stop em?"

"Jasper...come here," Obediah took his reluctant friend by the arm and walked to the edge of the camp. "Hollerin' at these young folks won't help. They're scared, alone, and probably lost. The only security they've got are wagon ruts to follow and one good storm will likely wash them out. They've hardly got a chance."

"Well, now, thet's exactly what I'm sayin'..."

"So?"

"So?" Jasper scratched his grizzled chin and stared hard at his companion. "Are you sayin what I think yer sayin'?"

"Well?"

"What?" hissed Jasper, with extreme exasperation."

"Why not?"

"Well...I...we...are yew plain crazy?"

"I don't think so, I..."

"Well, I'm beginnin' to. We've spent weeks gettin' this far and if we turn around now and get loaded down with these pilgrims we not on'y won't get t' Saint Louie, we might jest get our hair lifted. In fact, I'd jest bet on it."

Obediah looked at his old friend. "You're right, Jasper. You're right as usual," he said turning back to the camp.

"Well...now...jest a minute or two," Jasper whispered loudly.

"Well, what? It's simple. They can catch up with the others or another bunch might catch up with them. They'll be all right."

"It ain't likely an' you know it," said Jasper. "They already told us the others had gone ahead months ago and it's too late in the year fer anybody with any sense at all t' be crossing the plains now. They're alone an' you know it as well as I do."

"Well?"

"Well, what?"

"What're we going t' do?"

***

"Wake up, young'n," said Jasper, as he rudely jabbed the sleeping boy in the ribs. "If'n yer determined t' be a pilgrim, be a good'n."

"Huh...what're we doin'?"

"We're gettin' up, that's what we're doin'," said Jasper, pulling Butch's blankets off of him.

"But I was..."

"I know what you was," said Jasper. "We've got t' get movin' an' I'm gonna need yer help. You look like the makin's of a real he b'ar if somebody jest points yer snout in the right direction."

Butch's attention immediately sharpened. "Ya mean me?"

"Sure I mean you. Who else?" Jasper turned and began walking off. "I sure don't see nobody else around here."

"Gosh...yessir," said the boy, struggling to pull his pants up and look as adult as possible. "What 're we gonna do?"

"Well sir, I need ya t' go get the horses an' get 'em hitched t' the wagon," Jasper said, turning and observing his young helper. "Ken ya do that?"

"Yessir." Butch was on the run.

"Hold on, young'n," hollered the old mountain man. "Jest hold on 'till I tell ya somthin'. Come over here, now."

"Yessir."

"Jest lookit out there."

Butch followed the mountain man's finger and peered into the silent, early morning blackness surrounding the camp. "Yessir."

"Whaddya see?"

"Nothin'."

"That's exactly right. Nothin'. No Indians. No nothin'. Wagh! How d' ya know they ain't out there jest waitin' ta lift yer hair?"

Butch swallowed. "Well...I..."

"Truth is, ya don't, do ya?"

"No, sir."

"Ain't yew a caution? Yew an' yer sisters out here on the plains. Yew ain't got no idea where ya are or what yer up against. Why if'n it weren't fer me an' Obediah Jones over there, yer hair'd be hangin' from some lodge pole before night fall."

"Gosh."

"Yew bet. Obediah an' me has cut Injun sign fer nearly a week now, and we've been comin' the direction yer goin'. So, what does that tell ya?"

"Well...gee..."

"That's exactly what it tells ya. Caution, boy...plumb caution if'n yer ever goin' t' see yer people again." Jasper took Butch by the arm and led him to the edge of the small dark camp. "Sun up ain't fer a while yet, but look out int' the darkness until ya can begin t' make out the outlines of trees and brush and things."

"Yessir."

"Stay low, and look fer things what somehow don't look right, or sounds that are out of place or sounds ya otta hear but don't."

Butch peered intently into the darkness surrounding the camp.

"Well," Jasper said, "Whaddaya think?"

"Gosh...I don't know."

"It'll come with time, boy. Jest always be mindful of it, ya hear?"

"Yessir."

"Things seem peaceable enough. Now, walk...don't run...down and get the horses. Don't spook 'em, an' always stay watchful."

The small boy blended into the blackness. "Yessir," he whispered.

The days swept by in a dusty blur, filled with problems and adventure. The nights were increasingly cold and told of the arrival of autumn. A sense of urgency was felt by everyone.

A special bond began to rapidly develop between Jasper Pughsey and Butch, and Jasper began to help the boy reach for young manhood.

Dark came quickly after a long day of travel filled with wagon trouble. The small party made camp in a shallow swale next to an almost dry creek bed lined with cottonwoods and willows.

Deborah stood up from the aromatic pot boiling at the side of the fire.

"Well...it doesn't look like much, but there's certainly more in that pot since those two mountain men joined us."

"Uh-huh...Here they come now, I think."

The two men entered the circle of fire light complaining about the day's problems, Butch following a short distance behind.

"Another day like this one and we never will get to the mountains," said Obediah.

"Yep, and if we do, there's no guarantee we'll make it up the first dry creek bed," said Jasper, crossing his legs and collapsing by the fire. "That purely smells divine, young lady, it surely does."

"Thank you," said Deborah, filling the plates. "Its getting cold enough at night now to make a stew taste real good."

"Truly."

Each took a plate and found a place near the fire. Overwhelmed by the delicious aroma and a great hunger, Jasper Pughsey got immediately to the business of eating.

"Mr. Pughsey, with all that has been happening since the two of you joined us we've neglected it, but it is our custom to ask a blessing on the food," said Deborah.

Jasper choked swallowing his mouthful of delicious stew. "It is? Yes, ma'am," he said, putting his plate on the ground beside him. "That's right thoughtful, ma'am," he said, assuming an air of piety obviously alien to him.

Except for the cheerful crackle of the fire, silence descended on the small camp.

"Well?" asked Deborah.

Jasper looked around in alarm, "Well?"

"Yes."

"Yew mean me, ma'am?"

"Would you be so kind?"

"Well...I...tarnation," Jasper muttered, awkwardly attempting to rise from his cross-legged position.

"You needn't stand, Mr. Pughsey."

Jasper collapsed into his former position with a thump, dust billowing from beneath him. Never had he been in so compromising a position. The irritation was almost beyond the limits of his endurance. In complete resignation, if not total defeat, he raised his hat straight in the air, his gray hair falling about his face and ears. "Almighty, bless this here food so's it don't p'ison none of us. That's all." Replacing his hat and grabbing his plate, he quickly began attacking his food.

"Amen," said Deborah. The others repeated
her in unison.

"Thank you," said Deborah.

"Yes'm."

"Yessir, Mr. Pughsey."   Butch's admiration
knew no bounds.

"At breakfast we'll ask Butch to do it like he's
been taught."

"Yes," said Jennifer, piously.

Obediah swallowed a tasty mouth full. "That
was a right thoughtful prayer, Jasper."

"Now, Obediah..."

"I never knew."

"Never knew what?" Jassper retorted irritably."

"Well...you're a man of hidden depths."

Buck and Nails struggled to pull the wagon
and its occupants up the steep incline to the top of the
low ridge. Both horses were showing the effects of
many long days on the prairie, but their spirits
seemed strong.

"Oh, will you just look at that," said Deborah.

"Oh, it is beautiful," Jennifer agreed.

The prairie seemed to roll ahead of them
forever, its blue-green grass waving restlessly in the
fresh wind.

Jasper Pughsey, with Butch mounted behind
him, galloped up beside the wagon and reined the
horse to a stop in a cloud of dust.

"Whoa," he said, reaching behind himself and
grabbing Butch by the arm. "Swing down, young'n.

"Yessir."

The two girls climbed down from the wagon.

"Ain't that a sight, though," said Jasper, as he dismounted and walked up to the two girls. "My stars, every time I see it, it purely thrills me."

"It's glorious." said Deborah.

"What is?" asked Butch.

Jasper looked around at Butch with a deep scowl of disapproval. "Youngster...I sware I don't know how you can walk around with yer eyes open and be sa blind. Look out there...it's life itself."

"Yessir."

"Look at that grass...and see...way out yonder? Them's buffler. And that ragged blue line way out on the horizon? Them's the Rocky Mountains...pure heaven itself, that's what."

Deborah shaded her eyes against the bright sun light. "You mean those are the mountains?"

"Yep. They surely are."

"They don't look very big," said Jennifer.

"And all we have to do is get through them and we'll be with our people?" asked Deborah.

"Well...I wouldn't put..."

"Where's the buffler?"

"Gettin' through 'em is gonna be a bit of a trial, girl."

"Yes," said Jennifer, "but we're almost there."

"Where's the buffler?"

"Mountains, canyons, gullies, bear, cats, and, worst of all, Indians. Why," said the mountain man, "we'll be there afore ya know it." Jasper looked around scratching his grizzled chin. "Obediah otta be gettin' back here afore long. Keep an eye out, ya hear?" he said, as he began tying his horse to the back of the wagon.

"Mr. Pughsey...where's the buffler?" Butch asked, scanning the wilderness before him.

"Oh, my stars, boy...lookit out there. See that black herd out yonder? All them black critters? Why there's sa many of em, how can ya miss 'em?"

"Oh, yessir," the boy said, filled with wonder.

"We'uns are gonna get us one tomorrow. And we'll have the most eleegant banquet you three ever set yourselves down to," said Jasper Pughsey, with relish.

"Oh, that will be grand," said Jennifer. "How do you fix them?"

"Leave that ta me, girl. I ain't about t' let no pork eatin' young'n spoil such a feast."

"I'm so tired, you can do all the cooking," said Deborah, climbing up to the wagon seat.

"Yep...I spect so. Lookit off yonder...that row of trees off yonder?"

"Yes...way out there?"

"Yep, them's the ones. We'll make camp there. There's likely water somewhere about. Let's move out. I'll betch ya we'll find Obediah somewheres around there jest a spyin' on us."

Jasper mounted his horse and galloped off into the abundant grass of the prairie.

Smelling water, Buck and Nails broke eagerly over the low ridge line. In a shallow swale, among some cottonwood and sycamore trees, flowed a small, meandering stream. The two thirsty horses pulled the wagon to the stream's edge and began to drink deeply.

Jasper rode up with a clatter. "Don't let 'em out there he hollered, there could be quick sand, and we'd never get 'em outta there."

Deborah climbed down from the wagon. "Butch, help us get these horses back, and we'll make camp."

"Yew help 'em, boy. I'm gonna scout around a bit an' see if'n I can find Obediah. When they get their full, stake them horses over there behind them bushes, under the trees yonder."

"Yessir."

Jasper let his horse drink and then reigned around and urged the horse to a fast trot up stream, quickly leaving his busy companions behind. The creek meandered slowly around trees and bushes at the bottom of the shallow gully, small dry creek beds feeding into the stream from the ridge. Jasper jabbed his heels into the horse's flanks and the animal clamored across the creek and clattered up the rockfall of a dry tributary. As the horse and rider lunged over the top of the embankment, Jasper saw Obediah coming at a fast gallop through the rolling, restless sea of prairie grass.

"Whoa." Jasper patted the neck of his horse. "Let's see what ol' Obediah Jones has got t' tell us. Seems he's in a bit of a hurry."

Obediah rode up, dust billowing around his lathering horse. "It doesn't look too good, Jasper...whoa, easy."

"Whaddaya mean?"

The two men dismounted and squatted in the dirt, allowing their horses to begin grazing lazily in the hot, late summer sun. Bees and flys buzzed in the sweet, abundant grass.

"Injun sign all over the place.   There's
Cheyenne behind us, a dozen or so, and I think
they're a hunting party."

"Probably headed north, don't ya think?"
asked Jasper.   "Seems like it's gettin' late in the
season..."

"Yes, but that's not what worries me the most."

"What?"

"Believe it or not...I cut Blackfoot sign out
yonder near the mountains."

"What? Can't be."

"That's what I thought, but it's true enough."

"But that jest don't make no sense at all. Last
we seen of them devils was up on the Snake or the
Yellowstone."

"Well...they're out there somewhere in front of
us now and as near as I can tell it's a big
encampment."

Jasper stood up stretching his cramped legs,
leaving his crouching friend studying the dirt at his
feet.

"What'll we do?"

"One good thing...they seem to be moving into
the mountains ahead of us. I expect they'll start
north toward their home grounds. Like you say, it's
late in the season for them, too."

"True enough, but like you said, them
Cheyenne's behind us, and they could be headin' our
way."

Obediah stood up and stretched. "Careful's the
word, old partner. Careful's the word."

"Well...I'd like ta jest light right outta here,
that's what."

"Can't do that now."

"I reckon."

"We're too few to fight and a long way to go."

The two men mounted their horses and headed back toward the small camp.

"Let's be as invisible as we can and still make headway."

Jasper scratched his chin. "Our possibles ain't none too plenty. One shot tomorrow fer a buffler, and we keep right on movin'."

"Right."

CHAPTER 13

The night was cold and the small fire gave warmth from the chill of the prairie wind. Butch and Jasper hunkered down near the fire with their heads close together. Jasper produced a small lead vial from the pocket of his buckskins. "Gimme yer hand, boy." Jasper hissed in a secretive manner.

"What is it?" Butch asked, as Jasper poured a small drop of clear, foul-smelling liquid into the boy's dirty, upturned hand.

"Boy," he hissed, "don't ye know nothin'?" The old man's eyes glistened in the fire light. "It's snake oil."

"Snake oil?" The boy jerked back his hand, his eyes wide, "What's it do?"

"Thet's sure enough powerful stuff, it is," Jasper growled. Surveying the camp to be sure no one else shared the importance of their secret, he said, "That stuff'll sure enough put hair on yer chest, and it'll cure jest about any other problem what ails ya."

"Yer kiddin'?"

"Would I do that?" Jasper whispered unbelievingly.

"Well...I dunno...."

"Sure enough mountain men use it all the time."

"No foolin'?"

"Why, oncet I even skerred some injuns with
it. They was out t' skin my hide and this stuff plumb
saved m'life."

"Really? How?"

"Well, sir...le' me think. As I recollect, I was
up north, around Coulter's Hell, and I was...," the
very name struck wonder in Butch's mind, "and I
was bein' chased by a bunch a Blackfeet, mebby eight
or ten of 'em. I knowed I was in a heap a trouble, fer
sure. If'n I didn't do somethin' quick, I was done
fer. They hates us whites." Jasper scratched his
bristly chin, "Well, sir, as I ran up a small canyon, I
ducked behind some boulders so's them injuns
wouldn't see me, an' I came face ta face with the
biggest, ugliest rattler you ever see'd in your borned
days."

Butch's eyes were wide with wonder and he had
forgotten the cramps in his legs.

Jasper leaned a little closer. "I didn't know
which t' face first, them injuns or that there rattler.
Howmsoever, knowin' what them Blackfeet'd do t'
me, I soon figgered that one out." Jasper leaned down
and quickly seized a twig by the fire, "I grabbed thet
old rattler behind 'is ugly head jest as 'e struck."

"Wow!"

"Yep, I surely did. Oh, he was mad. He rapped
his se'f around my arm with his ol' buzzer jest a
goin' and them fangs a his fairly drippin'. Ya
never see'd the likes of t. Well sir, I hooked them
fangs a his over the edge a that ol' tin cup a mine and
milked that ugly critter dry. Then I flang 'im down
the mountain side right about where I figgered them
injuns t' be when I'd need 'im again the most."

"What'd ja do? Where was the injuns?" the boy whispered excitedly.

Looking around against possible intrusions, Jasper patted the excited youngster on the shoulder. "Shish, keep it down, boy. Keep it down. Ya don't want them women out here a clackin' at us, do ya?"

"No sir," the boy said looking around.

Jasper leaned back on his heels, and said, "This here ain't the kind a information a genuine mountain man'll give t' jest anybody. This is one a them there pure secrets what's past by word a mouth amongst the true giants of the mountains, y' know."

"Gosh," Butch whispered with wonder.

"Well, sir." Jasper shifted his weight. "I mixed that p'ison with the other secret ingredients, all of which is necessary fer pure snake oil, and rubbed it on m' chest an' arms. By now them injuns was a workin' their way up the canyon a lookin' fer me enney place they figgured I'd likely be. So's I snucked around so's I was up wind from 'em." The old man snickered. "You never seed the likes of 't. The canyon breeze took the smell a this here oil down t' them injuns and you never seed such a worried bunch a red skins in your young life. They knowed it was bad medicine fer sure." Jasper cleared his throat. "Well sir, about the time they figgured the spirits was comin' fer 'em sure, one of 'em stepped right smack in the middle a that big rattler. Thet snake was purely mad, havin' jest gone through the indignity of loosin' his p'ison, and' bein' throwed on the rocks, an' all."

"Oh, yeah," the boy agreed seriously.

Jasper leaned closer, "Thet bunch a Indians was nothin' but arms an' legs an' bug eyes an' wide open mouths. You ain't never heered such a noise in

your young life. They was runnin' int' each other,
an' fallin' over rocks an' grabbin' an kickin', an'
that ol' snake was right in the middle of 'em. It was
the biggest show I seen since the pigs ate Uncle
Shucks."

"Whudja do?" Butch asked, with the wonder of
a true worshiper.

"Whud I do?" Jasper responded in surprise.
"Well sir, ma first reaction was t' step int' that mob
an' whip ever' one of 'em. But bein' not only a man
of uncommon courage and stren'th, I took mercy on
them injuns and decided they had enough troubles. I
scrambled up the scree an' over the ridge."

"I'll bet them injuns are still wonderin' what
hit 'im." Butch said, his eyes gleaming.

"You betcha, boy," Jasper said, leaning closer.
"Now," he continued, in a serious tone, "I'm goin' t'
give ya some of this here stuff t' keep safe." Jasper
pulled a small bottle with a cork stopper from the
pouch at his belt and poured some of the foul liquid
into it. "Keep this fer real emergencies," he said,
putting the stopper tightly in its place, "fer real
emergencies. It's sure enough powerful stuff."

"I'll say."

"Remember...real emergencies."

The boy took the small mysterious and
wonderous jar from this great mountain benefactor,
"When's that?"

Jasper peered over his shoulder out into the
dangerous night. "Might be any time, so's ya
always want t' keep it close."

"Like where?"

"I keep mine right here," Jasper said, holding
the small leather pouch that hung from his belt.

"Gee, where can I get me a pouch like that, Mr. Pughsey?" asked Butch. "I really need one."

"Well...lesee," Jasper said, rubbing his gristled chin as though in serious thought. "Mebby I got a extry one amongst m' possibles. You wait here, boy." Jasper got up and walked silently to the wagon where the two mountain men had stashed their saddles and belongings.

Butch watched this great hero of the west fumble among his possessions. Boy, I sure hope he's got one, he thought.

The night was cold and silent except for the wind and the distant call of a wild bird. A moment later the answer of its mate came from somewhere in the darkness near the camp. Jasper's head came up, his senses alert.

"You wait here, boy. Don't ya' move," he said quietly from his spot near the wagon. Silently, the big man disappeared in the darkness surrounding the small camp.

Only if told by Jasper Pughsey would Butch stay in one place. Somehow, the small fire radiated security from its dying embers and the boy huddled closely over it.

Jasper moved in a crouch through the deep prairie grass and into the trees near the camp. The only sound he made was the undetectable hissing of his moccasins through the damp grass. Crouching near a tree, he could see the silhouettes of the two big horses against the star-filled expanse of black sky. "Too dadburned quiet," Jasper muttered to himself, his senses alert to the slightest intrusion, "Somethin's wrong somewheres."

Suddenly, one of the big horses jerked his head up and blew, shying to one side. Jasper slipped through the grass to one of the black trees to which the hitching rope was tied, securing the two horses. From this vantage point, one of the horses appeared to have six legs, two of them human. Indians, he thought to himself. We ain't got enough troubles, I jest knowed they'd get here sooner or later. Lessee...how many.

Jasper studied the night. The Indian slowly rubbed the big horse with one hand, calming him as he moved toward the rope which secured the animal. On'y one, I reckon, Jasper thought. Moving as silently as possible, his sound muffled by the night breeze, Jasper ran to the side of the horse and dived beneath it grabbing the unsuspecting Indian by his ankles and yanking him roughly to the ground beneath the startled horse. In panic the horse began to rear and plunge as Jasper and the Indian rolled beneath him. Hooves seemd to fill the air as the frightened horse tried to flee the sudden danger.

The Indian's knife was out before his back had hit the ground, but surprise gave Jasper the advantage. Lunging on top of the Indian, grabbing the slashing knife and forcing the point around beneath him, Jasper buried it deeply in the straining Indian's side. The red man struggled briefly and then went limp, the knife slipping into the dust.

Gathering the knife, Jasper pulled the Indian from beneath the horse and into the tall grass. He studied the knife and then looked closely at the dead Indian. "Blackfoot...they's gotta be more of 'em. Too fer east fer jest one," he muttered to himself.

"You can bet on it," said Obediah Jones.

"Wha... Damnation, where'd you come from? I thought you was asleep, sure."

"I never sleep."

"Then where was ya when I needed ya."

"Right here."

"What?"

"You did just fine, Jasper. I knew the minute I saw ya there'd be no problem with this fellow."

Jasper grew indignant. "Yew mean you was right here all along an' I coulda been kilt?"

"Well, I was about to grab him when you stepped in and saved me all that bother."

"Well, if that don't beat all. Why...man...if I..." Jasper sniffed the air. "What's that smell?"

"Whew...I don't know...something dead?"

Butch's small, black form bobbed between the trees. "Mr. Pughsey, Mr. Jones I heard the ruckus and I..."

"Boy, what's that you've got on ya...where've you been?" asked Obediah, putting out his hand to stop the boy's closer approach.

"Why, it's snake oil," Butch said proudly.

"Snake oil?"

"Oh, oh," Jasper said, turning toward the camp.

"Uh-huh, snake oil. Mr. Pughsey gave it to me fer when there's trouble, and when I heard the horses I knew I'd better use it."

"Snake oil?" Obediah looked at Jasper.

"Well, you used it, you surely did," Jasper said, grabbing the boy by the shoulder and turning back toward camp, away from Obediah.

"Snake oil, Jasper?"

"Snake oil, Obediah...you know," he hissed, waiving Obediah away. Jasper pulled the small boy behind him and moved quickly toward camp. "Yew gotta get that stuff off'n ya, now the trouble's over,

boy. It's meant jest fer yer enemies, not yer
friends."

"But you said..."

"I know...I know, an' ya done real good, too.
Thet's probably what give me the edge back there."

"Gee, ya really think so?"

"Uh-huh...no doubt in my mind."

"No doubt," said Obediah, following the two
into camp.

"Now, Obediah.... Ya didn't use it all up did
ya, boy?"

"No sir."

"That's good...you seen what an effect it has."

"Yessir."

"Devastation."

"Yessir...but what if there's more Indians out
there," Butch asked, motioning to the darkness
surrounding the camp.

"Oh, they's out there a'right, ya can count on it.
Thet one was tryin' his best t' run off the horses, then
we'd be fixed, sure."

Jasper poured water from his canteen into a
large coffee pot Obediah had brought from their cash
of possibles in the wagon.

"Whew...boy, when that water boils, wash that
stuff off'n ya."

"But if there's more Indians..."

"Don't yew worry none about that, boy," said
Jasper, putting more small pieces of wood on the fire,
"like I told ya, thet's fer pure emergencies."

"Yessir."

Jasper left the fire and the boy and walked over
to Obediah who had returned to the wagon. "I'm
thinkin' on lookin' around some. Could be that
Blackfoot was alone, but more'n likely there was two

'r three others around on a scoutin' expedition,"
Jasper said, scratching his balding head.

"That's a good idea. Too far east for just one.
I'll stay here and keep the lid on things if they come
back before you do. You suppose that boy can use a
rifle?"

"I reckon. It was you he gave such a rousin'
welcome to," Jasper grinned. "I had t' save ya from
'im, remember?"

"That's why I asked."

"Uh-huh. I reckon with a little learnin' in the
finer ways, he could be considerable help. Least
way's he's gonna have a chance t' learn."

"Yes...I'll talk to him.

"I'll be back right soon." Jasper's stalky form
melted into the late-night darkness as Obediah
returned to the fire.

Jasper moved back toward the horses a few
yards from the wagon. Approaching the horses, he
sensed something was wrong, but he could not
identify the source of his anxiety. Then it came to
him, the Indian's body was gone.

Jasper studied the ground. "I kilt 'im, sure,"
he mumbled to himself, "he couldn't of crawled off.
Gotta be some more around here some place."

Jasper found the spot where the Indian had been
lying. The grass had not yet sprung back and Jasper
could see where the body had been dragged away.
The mountain man turned and trotted back to camp.

Jasper found Obediah by the fire. Sitting down
beside his friend, he said, "Looks like ma'be two 'r
three others carried 'im off."

Well, if that's the case, we could be in some
trouble."

"A passle, sure."

"What'll we do?" asked Deborah, approaching the fire.

"Come mornin', we'll make tracks fer the mountains," said Jasper.

"But I thought we was goin' buffler huntin'," Butch interrupted.

"You'll get your chance," said Obediah.

"We'll make camp early tomorrow afternoon, boy," said Jasper, "and afore you ken shake a stick, you an me'll have us a fat cow, fer sure."

"We'll have us some meat and by the next day we should be fairly close t' Fort Laramie, and then we're into mountain country."

"Gosh, a real fort?" enthused Butch.

"Does that mean a bath and a chance to wash some clothes?" asked Deborah.

"Ain't likely," said Jasper. Not much there nowadays. It's mostly in ruin, but we can take some time t' do what ya need. It's safer there. Bordeaux and some of his men still try t' do business there."

"After weeks of what you've been through, it might seem like civilization to you," said Obediah. "We'll need to cross the Platte there and that can be kind of tricky."

"May not amount ta much this time a year."

"Maybe not."

"Right now, we got us some injuns t' worry about," said Jasper. "There's a bunch somewhere real close."

"What'll we do?" asked Deborah.

"You two women get in the wagon and try t' get some sleep," responded Jasper. "Us three men'll watch fer them redskins."

"Yeah," said Butch.

Jasper grabbed a blanket. "You slip under this blanket and get under the wagon there behind the wheel with yer rifle where ya ken pertect yer sisters. Them injuns'll never think of ya under there."

"Yessir."

"Be watchful," warned Jasper.

"Yessir."

Jasper returned to the fire. "He'll be asleep afor' I ken spit."

"Yes...he's a real fighter," sighed Obediah.

"No need t' worry t'night," said Jasper. "I think we gave 'em somethin' t' ponder on."

"I think you're right but let's both sleep with one eye open. We need to get movin' as early as we can."

CHAPTER 14

Butch felt as though he were standing chest deep in an endless, waving sea with the cool wind blowing long graceful waves toward him.

"See there, boy?" Jasper pointed off toward the blue line of mountains on the western horizon. "Do ya see 'em?"

"Uh..."

"Buffler, boy! Buffler," Jasper said, taking Butch's head in his hands and pointing the boy's nose in the appropriate direction.

"I don't see nothin', Mr. Pughsey."

"If'n yer ever gonna be a genuine mountain man, the least ya gotta do is learn ta spot buffler when they ain't up close." Jasper scowled at his young, worshipful companion. "I mean that's the absolute least. Wagh!"

Jasper pointed toward the horizon. "Look at 'em. See 'em?"

"Oh...yeah," Butch said, astonished at his success. "I see 'em...I see 'em...let's go!" Butch took off into the tall grass of the great American prairie.

"Hold on, youngster," Jasper said, grabbing the boy by the collar of his shirt. "Ya gotta do it right, boy, or there'll be nothin' but grass when ya get there."

Jasper tested the wind. "Come on," he said, and began trailing through the tall grass.

"Mr. Pughsey, why don't we ride our horses? It seems like a ways off."

"Don't need no horses, boy. They'll jest faller us along kind a unnoticeable like. If'n we go ridin' in there like thunder on the mountain, them ol' buffler'll be gone afore ya can say scat."

"Oh..."

"We don't want ta spook that herd, now do we?"

"No, sir."

"We gotta stay down wind from 'em an' do nothin' ta startle 'em when we get nearer."

"Boy, I sure hope we get one, we surely need it."

Jasper stopped and looked disdainful and imperious, "You doubtin' me, boy?"

"No...sir."

"Then hesh up and learn."

Unexpectedly, the prairie split into a gully that had been invisible in the deep grass.

"This way, boy."

"Yessir."

The gully ran for several hundred yards into the middle of the buffalo herd and flattened out to merge once again with the level prairie.

"Hesh, boy, we gotta be quiet er we'll startle 'em."

"Yessir."

Jasper crouched in the grass, the boy next to him. The herd was grazing peacefully all around them. "Which one er we gonna get, Mr. Pughsey?"

"Shh."

Jasper's big Hawkin was right in front of Butch's nose.

"Butch, these is shinin' times, boy."

"Huh?"

"Shinin' times, boy. See that fat cow right there?"

Butch looked indiscriminately among the huge animals, "Yeh," he lied.

"Thet's the one what's goin' in our stew pot, yew bet."

"Yessir," the boy said eagerly.

Slowly, Jasper brought the big Hawkin to his shoulder. "Thet, fat cow'll be in our pot right soon."

Butch held his breath.

Jasper's shoulder jumped violently with the roar of the huge rifle.

"He's still there, Mr. Pughsey," Butch said, in disbelief, "but I saw where ya hit 'im...the dust flew up."

Jasper chuckled, "Jest you watch, young'n."

With the impact of the large lead ball, the big cow had trotted forward a few feet and stood rigidly still. The other animals in the herd, with the exception of those closest to the cow, paid little attention to the fate of their great hairy companion.

"Don't move, boy."

"Yessir."

"Lookit 'er nose, boy."

"What...is it blood?"

"Yep, sure nuff. Ain't these shinin' times, boy? It's gonna be hump roast t'night, fer sure."

The big cow seemed to stand taller, and then its rigid legs began to slowly spread, blood now spilling profusely from its nose and mouth. The cow jumped forward a few paces and slowly toppled over on its side in the dust, its legs remaining perfectly stiff. The huge beast fell like a tree having been cut at the base. Butch almost wanted to yell timber as it fell.

"Wait, boy."

Jasper slowly stood up and studied the prairie.

"What's a matter?"

"You think maybe somebody 'sides them buffler mighta heered this here old Hawkin?"

Jasper had felt uneasy for several days, now. He knew a run in with Indians could not be avoided much longer.

Butch's cramped legs were beginning to hurt.

"Okay, let's go get dinner."

Butch started off at a run.

"Hold on, boy," Jasper said, grabbing the eager boy by the shoulder. "Ya don't go runnin' up on a shot buffler thataway."

"How come?"

"Oh...boy...," Jasper exclaimed, with a pained look of pure exasperation. "Don't y' know nothin'? What if'n that buffler ain't dead?"

"Oh...yeah..."

"Ya gotta be kerful, boy. Things ain't always what they seem in the wilderness. Look everywhere and look hard. Seein' ain't always thet easy, boy. Ya gotta look b'fer y' ken see."

"Yessir."

The alternative's bad, boy. Real bad. Injuns come outta nowheres, snakes hit ya when ya coulda swarn there weren't none, dead buffler jump up and gore ya open."

Cautiously, Jasper approached the huge beast and poked at it with his rifle. The buffalo was dead, a single shot through its lungs.

"I ain't gonna show ya this but once, boy. Come 'ere."

"Is 'e dead?"

"Yep."

Butch cautiously approached the buffalo.

"Oh, boy...come here," Jasper said, motioning at the reluctant boy. "This here buffler's plumb dead," he said, poking at the dead animal.

"Now this ain't gonna be no easy trick fer no pork eater, even with my help."

"What's a pork eater?"

"Now...what we gotta do is get this cow on 'er belly with 'er legs out straight so's she don't roll on us...got it?"

"Yessir. Ah...what's a pork eater?"

"Ferget it. Now, we gotta get these two bottom legs folded up again' 'er body," Jasper said, seizing the front and hind legs nearest the ground. "You hold 'em in again' the body...like so, an' I'll try t' roll 'er on 'er belly. Got it?"

"Yessir."

"Hold 'em like so."

Butch took the two hooves and, pulling the front one back and the back one forward, pushed them against the belly of the dead beast.

From the other side of the cow, Jasper leaned down and put his shoulder into the spine of the huge animal and said, "Now...I'm gonna roll 'er over towards ya, so watch yerself...Okay?"

"Okay."

Jasper leaned hard into the buffalo and, grabbing huge clumps of shaggy, brown hair, lifted up in an effort to roll the heavy, dead cow on its stomach. Dust filled the air and settled in their hair and on their faces.

"Uh...Mr. Pughsey?"

"Huh? Oh...land sakes, what is it now, boy?" Jasper grunted.

"What's a pork eater?"

Jasper's face appeared above the furry carcass and glared at his young companion. "Don't ask no dumb questions, young'n. We gotta concentrate an' get outta here."

"Yessir," said Butch, pressing the cow's hooves against her belly with renewed vigor.

Slowly, the dead beast rose up from the ground. It seemed for a moment to Butch that it had come to life and was attempting to get to its feet.

"Watch it, boy."

"Yessir," Butch grunted.

"Now...when she's almost up, you put yer shoulder again' 'er so's she don't roll over on ya."

With one last effort, the beast was nearly on its stomach.

"Now...pull those legs out straight...quick and pull!"

"Yessir."

Butch grabbed the two big legs as they rolled toward him and pulled. The huge buffalo settled on its stomach, effectively spread eagled.

Jasper stretched his cramped back and drew his Green River knife from its scabbard. "Now, here goes, boy. Watch real careful."

"Yessir."

Jasper worked quickly and professionally, making a deep cut across the nap of the buffalo's neck, forward of the front quarters. Then he made a deep incision the full length of the animal's spine, his hand and arms soon covered with blood.

"What's a matter, boy?"

Butch looked pale.

"Well...I don't feel so good." Butch gulped hard.

From where the two incisions crossed, Jasper
began cutting the hide away from the meaty carcass.

"Yew was askin' what a pork eater was," he
said, absorbed in his work.

"Yessir."

"Well...that's what one is."

"What?"

"A squeemish city slicker what don't know
poor bull from fat cow and cain't expect t' survive on
the plains."

Under Jasper's sure knife, the cow was soon
denuded, its hide spread beneath it like a ground
cloth. Dismemberment came quickly. "We want
the hump and ribs...oh, that's truly good, and the best
is yet t' come."

Jasper rolled the dismembered buffalo over
and with a single, deft incision, cut open its belly,
and pulled its entrails from the body. "We gotta take
the boudins and liver."

"Why?" asked the increasingly pale boy.

"Boy...if'n yer bent on bein' a true mountain
man, yew gotta understand these things."

"Yessir," replied the chastised Butch.

"These," Jasper said, pulling the entrails free,
"constitutes the finest eatin' in the whole of
creation."

"They do?"

"Next t' the liver."

"The liver?"

"Yep," Jasper's head almost disappeared into
the hollow carcass, "the liver...oh my stars," his
hollow voice reverberated.

Butch stood transfixed, his face a mask of
disbelief as Jasper straightened up, his face covered

with blood. In his hand was a slimey mass of red, blood-covered gore.

"Oh, ain't these shinin' times, boy? Here, have some," he said, shoving the dripping mess in Butch's face.

Butch cringed. "What is it?" he said, struggling to control his convulsing stomach.

"Liver."

"Liver?"

"Yep...liver."

"But...it's raw."

"Yep." Jasper tore at the bloody liver, swallowing huge bites, hardly stopping to chew. "This here's mountain queezeen, young'n. Nothin' finer nowheres." Jasper stopped to chew a mouthful.

"First thing a mountain man wants after he's kilt his se'f a buffler is that nice, warm liver 'fore it gets cold. Here...have some."

Butch's stomach turned over, "Mountain men love it, huh?"

"Yep," Jasper responded, his mouth full. "Onliest thing what makes it better...lookit here..." he said, bending over the gaping, bloody carcass. "Thet's bile...dip it in there.... Oh, my stars, ain't nothin' in this whole world wat's any better." Jasper ate with true relish, his other hand, filled with steaming liver, extended toward Butch.

Butch swallowed hard as Jasper filled his hand with an oozing mass of warm, mucid liver.

"Take a bite, boy," Jasper said, chewing vigorously. Get that int' ya and ya'll know one of the true delights of the mountains...here...dip it in here."

Butch dipped the dripping liver into the dark, steaming bile inside the carcass. "This makes it better, huh?" he asked.

"Yew bet, boy," Jasper said, smacking his lips with relish and taking another mouthful. "Next, we gotta cut out the tongue."

"The tongue?"

"Uh-huh."

"What for?"

"Well, boy," Jasper said, wiping his mouth with his buckskin sleve," thet's the most wonderful part. When its been roasted in the hot coals of yer fire, it's the most delicate thing yew ever ate in your young life. So soft, so sweet...it excites pure rapture in the bosom, boy. It'll do it even fer a greenhorn."

"Gee."

"Now eat that liver like a man, afore it gets cold."

"Yessir."

Butch swallowed hard and looked at the steaming, dripping mass in his hands, then he looked at Jasper Pughsey. He knew if he didn't eat the liver, this giant of the mountains would no longer look upon him as a true companion...a side kick...a future mountain man like himself. He would always be considered a...a...a pork eater...a greenhorn.

Jasper walked around the carcus to the dead buffalo's head and began prying its stiffening mouth open with his knife. "Ain't that good, boy?"

"Ugh."

"Whasat, boy?" Jasper did not look up, but busied himself with removing the animal's tongue.

With grim determination to join the ranks of the truly initiated, and to win the everlasting admiration and further confidence of his great friend, Butch raised the cooling liver to his mouth and took a hesitant bite, but the liver going down met

Butch's breakfast coming up. Butch gagged, but managed to swallow everything and hold it down. It took great determination.

"Whasat?" asked Jasper, still working to remove the stubborn tongue. "Yew say somethin'?"

"No, sir," said Butch, his courage growing. The liver, though a bit tough, really didn't taste all that bad. In fact, with some determination, not to mention the encouragement of his hero, the liver could actually, possibly, be as good as Jasper seemed to think it was.

Butch turned to take another bite and froze. A line of mounted Indians sat silently along a low ridge not far from where Butch and Jasper were butchering the buffalo.

"Mr. Pughsey...."

"Ain't that good, boy. Oncet ya get that first bite down, it becomes somethin' wonderful, don't it, boy?"

"Mr. Pughsey...."

"Yew bet it does...there she is," said Jasper Pughsey, holding up the large tongue for Butch to see. "See there?"

"Mr. Pughsey...look." Butch seemed frozen in his place, his face as pale as if he had seen a ghost. In fact, he was looking at something far more frightening.

From the look on Butch's face, Jasper knew there was real trouble. Slowly, he turned and saw the menace on the nearby ridge.

"Mr. Pughsey..."

"Hesh, boy. Don't move." Jasper slowly slid his knife under his shirt and into the scabbard next to his skin. "We're in big trouble...but I been in worse."

"Aren't they...friendly?"

"No they ain't. Them's Bug's Boys...stay right still."

"What's Bug's Boys?"

Jasper let the tongue he had been holding fall to the ground. "Ol' Bug's the Devil...Satan...and these is his children, fer sure. They's Blackfeet and ain't nothin' they hate worse'n whites."

One of the Indians urged his poney forward a few paces, separating himself from the others. In his left hand was a large war club.

"Yew stay by me now, boy. No matter what happens, keep yer head and maybe we'll keep our hair."

"Yessir."

Jasper glanced at his Hawkin lying across the carcus slightly out of reach. "If'n I go fer that ol' bull thrower, we'd be dead afore I could reload, as fast as I am. There's jest too many of 'em."

"What's gonna happen?" asked Butch, trying to sound brave.

"I think 'e jest wants ta count coup. Then maybe they'll jest leave us alone."

"What's count coup?"

"My goodness," Jasper said impatiently, "yer jest full a questions at a bad time. He's gonna try t' hit me with that club. Not kill me, jest hit me."

"Why?"

"Why, that's big medicine among Bug's Boys. If'n they can touch an enemy without killing 'im or bein' killed, they can brag long and loud around their camp fires fer months t' come."

Suddenly, the Indian let out a blood curdling whoop and charged toward the two helpless companions.

"Remember, boy...and it's important...don't show no fear...no matter what. If'n they kill me and take you captive, be brave and always independent. That's all they'll ever respect."

"Yessir...look out, Mr. Pughsey!"

The screaming brave charged head long into the two helpless friends. Jasper raised his arm and ducked to avoid the vicious blow, but the heavy club glanced off the side of his head. To Butch the crack of the club on Jasper Pughsey's head seemed to reverberate off the rocks and ledges of the nearby bluffs.

Jasper lay in a broken heap at Butch's feet, his head bleeding badly. Crys of victory came from the Indians at the top of the hill and they began advancing in a line toward Butch.

CHAPTER 15

The lodge was dark and smelled of pine smoke from the last night's fire. In the center of the roomy circle, a small but persistent trail of smoke floated up into the peak of the lodge where cobwebs of the past winter's smoke hung lazily among the lodge poles in the early morning darkness. Through the smoke hole, the brilliant stars in the dark sky were beginning to fade. Soon the sun would edge above the surrounding hills and filter through the pines in a lustrous display of color and life.

Butch had been awake for several hours listening to the birds come awake and fill the darkness with their noisy chatter in anticipation of the day ahead. Ordinarily, it would have been a sound of great joy and renewed life, but not this morning. His arms were numb from the buckskin straps that secured his wrists tightly behind his back.

It had been a miserable night. After the fire had died down the lodge had become cold and the ground was hard and uncomfortable through the single buffalo robe spread beneath him. Last night, after the Blackfoot victory dance, his captors had dragged him and Jasper Pughsey into the lodge and unceremoniously thrown them on the ground. The screeching, hollering, and gesturing of the victory dance and his dark captivity in the smoky lodge had almost been more than he could endure.

From the moment the Blackfoot brave had clubbed Jasper Pughsey down and had roughly taken Butch captive, he knew with the assurance of the condemned that he was going to die. Butch's despair had increased throughout a night filled with fear and fitful sleep. No one knew where he and Jasper were, and even if Obediah Jones could track them to the spot where they had killed the buffalo, the milling herd would have obliterated their sign. The Blackfoot braves had even finished butchering the cow and had brought most of the meat with them. They seemed highly resentful that Jasper and Butch had slaughtered it to begin with.

Butch wondered what Jennifer and Deborah were doing. How would they ever get to the Great Basin without him? They might even die on the plains but, then, Mr. Jones would surely help them. Jasper Pughsey had never paid that much attention to the girls, anyway, and even seemed to resent them. Butch felt some pride when he realized that it was he whom the great mountain man had taken a liking to and was teaching the ways of the mountains. He also knew that if he ever needed those skills, he needed them now.

Butch rolled over to relieve the pain and pressure in his arms. Squinting into the darkness he tried to make out Jasper Pughsey's features. Somewhere outside a squirrel chattered at some early morning intruder and Jasper Pughsey opened his eyes.

"Oh...Mr. Pughsey..."

"Hesh, boy."

"But..."

"Hesh up. Now's no time fer chatter. My ol' head's 'bout t' split wide open and we gotta figger a way outta here fast."

"Yessir," Butch whispered.

"If'n these injuns make up their minds about us, we're in a heap a trouble, fer sure. I don't remember nothin', boy. What's happened to us?"

"They dragged us t' their camp," Butch whispered, "threw us in here, and then they had a big celebration that sounded like it went on forever."

Jasper began struggling with his bindings. "How far are we from where we kilt the buffler?"

"Gee...I don't know."

"Well, how long did it take us t' get here, boy. Stop an' think."

Butch thought hard. "Maybe two or three hours...I was so scared...."

"I know, boy, and with good reason, too. Did ya move pretty fast?"

"No sir...not really. They made me walk...and I had t' run some or they'd have dragged me."

"Keep yer voice low, boy."

"Yessir."

"Did we cross any rivers?"

"Yessir...not too far from here."

"A big one?"

"Well...pretty big."

"Hmm..." The knot in the rawhide cut into Jasper's wrists and seemed to get tighter as he struggled to free himself. "Was it deep?"

"No, sir...I waded it. It got up t' my waist and it was cold and fast, but I made it."

"Yew surely did, boy. Yew surely did." Jasper smiled at the boy to encourage him. "You're purely the ha'r a the b'ar, boy, you purely are."

Butch's eyes grew wide. "Is that good, Mr. Pughsey?"

Jasper struggled with his bindings. "The best in the mountains, boy," he hissed with the effort. "Ya can't do much better than that."

"Gee."

"But we gotta do somethin' fast, er we're gonners."

"Yessir...but what."

"I'm thinkin', boy, I'm thinkin'...an' my head's purely killin' me."

Jasper struggled harder with his stubborn bindings and said, "Roll over with yer back t' me, boy."

"Huh?"

"Roll over back t' back...like this," Jasper said, rolling his back to Butch. "Lemme see if I can loosen yer wrists. One of us has gotta get loose enough ta untie the other."

Jasper struggled to loosen the rawhide bindings around Butch's wrists.

"Doggon, boy, I ain't havin' no luck. Yer fingers 're smaller 'n mine, you try."

"Yessir."

Butch struggled with the tight leather straps. "Mr. Pughsey, the knot's so small and tight, I can't seem t' get hold of it..."

"I know, boy...how long did that dancin' and hollerin' go on last night?"

"I don't know...I musta fell asleep, but I guess it was pretty late."

"I surely hope so, boy, I surely do."

"How come, Mr. Pughsey?"

"It's startin' t' get light an' we ain't outta here yet. The longer them injuns are asleep, the better."

"Ugh...what's that smell, Mr. Pughsey?"

Jasper sniffed the air and a wide grin lit his face. "That's salvation, boy. It surely is, that's pure salvation."

The skin covering of the lodge buldged inward between the supporting lodge poles above their heads and snapped back into place with a drum-like thump as a knife point pierced it and cut slowly and silently down to the ground. The hide covering parted and a huge, dark, redolent figure crawled noiselessly into the lodge.

"Grunt," hissed Jasper excitedly, "I don't know when I ever been sa glad ta see nobody."

"Ugnh."

The big Indian worked quickly cutting the leather thongs that bound the two captives' wrists and ankles.

"But old friend, yew surely don't smell no better. Worse, in fact. But right now," Jasper said, rubbing his wrists and ankles, "its pure ambrosia, it surely is...ain't it, boy?"

Butch nodded in an effort to look enthusiastic and fought to keep tears back. The pain was intense as the blood flowed back into his hands and feet, and he could not seem to get to his feet.

"Rub 'em, boy...like this...fast like...and pretty soon the hurtin' 'll stop."

The boy sank back on the robe. "Yessir."

"Ugnh." A massive, effluvious arm encircled Butch's waist and he was yanked off the ground with no warning and little apparent sympathy. With Butch tucked under his arm, Grunt slipped quietly through the gash in the buffalo hide covering of the lodge. Jasper followed quickly.

Outside, the two men stood silently sensing their surroundings.   The camp still slept. Somewhere a dog began to bark and another answered from the other side of the large encampment.

"I surely hope you know where t' go," Jasper said, "because I purely don't."

"Ugnh."

"Can I get down? My ribs hurt awful," Butch hissed.

"Hesh, boy. This here's pretty serious," Jasper whispered. "We get caught now, ol' Bug's Boys'll skin us alive fer sure."

The large Blackfoot encampment stood in a spacious meadow surrounded by forested mountains. The lodge in which Butch and Jasper were held captive was on the outer edge of the encampment and stood about fifty yards from the tree line. The grass was deep and smelled sweetly; it was covered with morning dew.

"Ugnh." Grunt pointed across the meadow.

"Yer right. Only one way ta do this," Jasper said, as the two moved quickly from the side of the lodge into the knee-high grass and headed for the nearest stand of pines.

"Mr. Pughsey," Butch gasped, the air being bounced out of his chest with every step taken by the fleeing Grunt.   "We're leaving an awful big trail."

Jasper looked over his shoulder at the two wide swaths in the trampled, wet grass.

"Looks like a herd a buffler 'sted a jest us," Jasper panted as they ran out of the wet grass and into the pines. "Maybe by the time they get ta stirrin', the sun'll burn the dew off and the grass'll spring back."

Jasper knew it was wishful thinking.

It was very hot, but a slight breeze played with the aspen and pines and the dappled shade felt cool to Obediah Jones. The mountain man stood well back from the sparse tree line studying the carcass of the fallen buffalo and the two horses grazing on the nearby prairie grass. His eyes swept the horizon and the ocean of gently waving prairie grass searching for clues as to what had happened. Some distance out on the prairie, Jasper's and Butch's horses grazed peacefully, but violence clung to the air like the smell of death. Laying in the hot sun, what was left of the buffalo carcass crawled with large, blue flies and it appeared to have been dead for some time. The breeze carried the stench to Obediah's nostrils.

The scene seemed undisturbed. The horses had not pricked their ears or shown any sign of nervousness since Obediah had first recognized them earlier in the day. Whatever danger had disturbed this place had passed.

Obediah stepped from the obscurity of the small stand of aspen and fir and walked cautiously out into the prairie grass, his rifle at the ready and his every sense alert to danger. As he drew near, the horses raised their heads and watched him as they contentedly chomped their grass. One stomped and blew, resentful at Obediah's approach, but neither horse moved.

The smell and the heat were oppressive and the flies buzzed loudly as they busied themselves over the

bloated carcass. Obediah felt sick, but walked up to
the buffalo and studied the details of the ground.

To the savvy mountain man, it was obvious
what had happened. Jasper Pughsey and Butch had
killed the buffalo, as they had set out to do, and were
enjoying some of the fresh meat when they were
overtaken by Indians.

Jasper wouldn't have left that tongue, Obediah
thought. The Indians, ten or twelve or so, had come
off the low ridge to the west and had apparently
overcome Jasper. There was too much buffalo blood
on the ground to determine how much might have
belonged to Jasper or Butch. But among the unshod
pony tracks leaving the scene and headed north were
Butch's unmistakable foot prints. The boy was
apparently unhurt—at the time, anyway.

"Must've happened about this time yesterday,"
Obediah mumbled to himself, scratching his chin.
"But why did they leave the horses," he wondered.

Obediah followed the tracks for a few yards to
the point where they turned northwest and headed
into the mountains.

"Doesn't look good," he said to himself,
"they're Blackfoot."

Obediah hurried back to his horse, tied in the
trees. Mounting, he rode out and gathered the other
two horses and started back to the camp at a slow trot.

"Mr. Jones, where do you think they are?"
asked Deborah.

"Don't worry, they'll be back." Obediah Jones
tried to cover his worry by busying himself in
packing camp gear. "We've got to break camp and
get moving. They'll catch up."

"Do you think they'll have more buffalo for us tonight?" Jennifer asked, as she climbed into the wagon with an armful of camp gear.

"Help Deborah with packing the rest of this stuff, while I hitch the horses," he said, a little too sharply.

"Yes, sir."

Obediah walked to where the horses were picketed and began the tedious job of harnessing the two big animals.

Deborah followed. "You know something, don't you?" she asked, hesitantly.

Obediah looked over Nail's broad back at the frightened girl. Swallowing hard, but trying to appear positive and in control, he said, "Yes...I think they may be in some trouble...."

"Oh, no."

"Well, now, just a minute," he said, in an effort to forestall tears. "Butch is with Jasper and he knows all of these mountains from one end to the other. Jasper was wandering around here outsmarting Indians before you were even borne."

"What's happened?" the girl asked, tears brimming her eyes.

"They killed buffalo yesterday. It appears from what sign I could make out that while they were skinning out the buffalo, they were surprised by Indians...Blackfoot."

"Blackfoot...are they bad?"

Obediah came around the harnessed horses and put his arm around the frightened girl. "Look...old Jasper knows what he's doing.... Here, help me get these horses back to the wagon. He won't let anything happen to Butch."

"But what if something awful has happened to Mr. Pughsey?"

"Now, nothing has happened to him in years. It hasn't now."

"But..."

"All right...I want to get you and Jennifer and the wagon up into those mountains as quickly as possible. Then I'll look for them. In fact, I've got a good hunch where those Blackfoot will be. Let's get 'em hitched and start moving."

"Where to?"

"If you stop talking and start helping, I can get us to Fort Laramie where you and your sister will be safe. Then I can get out and find your brother and Jasper and be of some help, if need be. And I don't think much will be needed."

"When will we get there?" Jennifer sighed.

"A day. Maybe two...depends."

"On what?"

"On everything...the horses, Indians, weather...just like you've seen since you left your home."

CHAPTER 16

Grunt let Butch to the ground when the three were well back into the trees some distance up the hillside from the camp.

"Oh, boy, thanks," Butch said with relief. "I don't about have any breath left in me."

Jasper sat down on a fallen log. "We're in trouble. Who knows how far we gotta go back ta where we can find Obediah, and I ain't got m' Hawkin. Without that ol' bull thrower, it ain't likely we'll get too far...."

"What'll we do, Mr. Pughsey?"

"Can't rightly say," Jasper said, scratching his grizzled beard. "All I got is ma knife."

"Ugnh," Grunt jestured further up the mountain and across a rocky draw in the mountain side.

"What?" Jasper responded. "What's that mean?"

"That's the way we came, Mr. Pughsey," Butch said. "I remember we came down that draw."

"Did, did ya?"

"Yessir."

"An' ya crossed the river on t'other side a that saddle in the mountain?"

"Yessir...that's it...I remember," Butch responded excitedly.

Jasper stood up grinning. "I'm goin' back fer ma Hawkin. We gotta ways ta go an' it's needful. Besides, I ain't no good with out it anyways."

"Ugnh!" Grunt waved his hand in front of his face in a negative gesture.

"I don't think he wants ya to go, Mr. Pughsey," Butch said.

"Well, ain't that jest too bad? Where's he think I'm gonna get me another cannon like the one them thievin' Indians stole?"

With many words and even more and profuse gestures, Jasper attempted to explain the nature of things to Grunt. When Grunt's protestations ceased, Jasper began to deal with the problem of finding his massive weapon.

"Now, Butch...stop an' think hard...."

"Yessir...."

"Did them injuns take my ol' bull thrower and my possibles?"

"Gosh...I was so scared...."

"Well, stop and think," Jasper said, trying to calm the boy's anxiety.

"Soon as we got to the camp they started hootin' an' dancin' and everything was pretty confused. But they took us right to the tent they kept us in."

"They didn't stop nowhere's else before?"

"No sir."

"Ya think that's were they might a throwed m' Hawkin an' stuff?"

"I dunno, but it's likely. They threw me in there an' then drug you in an' threw in a bunch a other stuff...I think yer gun was among it...I was pretty scared."

"Good boy," Jasper said clapping the boy on the back. "I'm gonna get that ol' bull thrower and we're gonna get outta here yet, but I gotta get it before them red devils realize what a prize they got."

"Yessir."

"Now Grunt...you take this young'n and head fer Fort Laramie. It can't be thet far. It's likely ya'll find Obediah Jones there with this boy's sisters. I jest know Obediah'll try an' get 'em there afore he tries ta come lookin' fer us. He'll want 'em off'n the open trail, least ways."

"Ugnh."

"Well...go on...get a goin'. You mind Grunt, now, ya hear?"

Without waiting for a response, Jasper turned and quietly decended through the trees toward the large Blackfoot encampment below.

Jasper reached the edge of the meadow in which the Blackfoot lodges were pitched and stopped to survey the scene. The gold of morning sunlight was beginning to splash among the tepee tops and the camp was coming to life. Further in the camp, among the lodges, two squaws were busying themselves with relighting a cook fire that had gone out during the night. The lodge in which Jasper and Butch had been kept captive stood only a short distance across the meadow. Crouching low, Jasper dodged from the tree line and through the deep, sweet smelling grass to the side of the lodge. The grass was still damp with early morning dew and Jasper's buckskin leggings stuck to his legs and the wetness seeped through his mocassins.

Silently the mountain man slipped through the hole Grunt had cut in the side of the tepee and into the dark, smokey interior of the lodge. His eyes searched the dim interior for the Hawkin and his bag of possibles.

"Oh, my stars above, there she is," he whispered to himself. The weapon and the remainder of his gear were piled near the tepee flap.

Grabbing his possessions, Jasper stooped through the hole in the side of the lodge and cautiously moved toward the now distinct trail in the deep grass. The sun was now up and filtering through the pine trees surrounding the camp, and the air was filled with the smoke of cooking fires renewed to meet the needs of the day. Jasper heard the increasing noise of the camp and knew he had to hurry.

Two braves emerged from a nearby lodge. One stretched and started walking toward the meadow, his companion, scratching his head and rubbing one sleepy eye, followed lazily. It was obvious to Jasper that they were going into the woods to relieve themselves and that they would soon see the trampled grass where he and his two companions had made their earlier escape. The mountain man was stuck and he knew it. If he ran he would immediately be seen; if he stayed where he was he would also probably be seen. His only realistic chance, as small as it was, was to stay put and hope for the best. As the two blackfoot braves drew closer, the mountain man flattened himself against the ground. He was well hidden in the grass and brush, but if he could have dug himself a deep hole, he would have eagerly done so.

The braves, absorbed in their chatter, started out into the deep grass. Suddenly the bigger one stopped short and studied the trails of trampled grass before him which led into the forest. The two gestured excitedly and turned and ran into the camp. Jasper could hear their cries of alarm sturring the camp to excitement as they disappeared between the nearby lodges.

Jasper, hesitating only a moment, realized that this was the chance he had hoped for, and grabbing his treasured Hawkin leaped from his hiding place in the grass and ran for the tree line across the meadow. The old mountain man knew that if he could only make it to the tree line he would probably be safe, but the treeline, though only yards away, seemed to be miles away and receded with every labored step Jasper took. He ran as swiftly as he could, but the tall grass seemed to grab at his moccasined feet and hold him to the damp earth. Lifting his feet high to avoid the grasping, clinging grass, the old mountain man bounded across the open expanse and into the forest. He had no sooner entered the dark, shaded safety of the treeline than havoc errupted from the Blackfoot camp. Jasper looked quickly over his shoulder to see a score of screaming, determined braves enter the meadow along his trail at full run.

Jasper Pughsey knew he was in for the fight of his life. He was alone, armed only with his knife and Hawkin, and the meanest enemy in the West was only a few yards behind him determined to reclaim their prize: most likely his hair. The old trapper's heart beat as if it would burst from his chest and his legs ran as if he had no control over them and they totally dominated his tired, aching body. As the mountain got steeper, Jasper clawed at the mountain side and scrambled almost on his hands and knees between the trees. His ears rang with the constant rush of his labored breathing and he felt as if his heart would burst. Suddenly the pine forest broke on the edge of a rocky talus in the mountain

side. The talus sloped steeply up to the ridge of the
mountain which, at some distant time past, had
crumbled and fallen.   Jasper stopped, his breath
coming in huge, ragged gulps. He could not see his
pursuers, but he could hear them scrambling and
tearing at the mountain beneath him. He had only
moments, and he knew it.

Rather than climbing out onto the unstable rock
slide where he would be in full view of the pursuing
Blackfeet, Japer began climbing along the brushy
side of the slide where the forest sought in vain to
reclaim the precipitous mountain side. The going
would have been easier and less demanding out on
the scree where the tired white man could defeat the
mountain one rock at a time, but he would have been
in full view of the oncoming enemy, an open,
alluring target for their arrows.

Struggling with the clawing, grasping brush,
Jasper finally pulled himself to the ridge line and
collapsed behind some of the larger bolders perched
precariously at the top of the crumbling mountain
side. The mountain man fought to get control of his
heaving, shaking body and peered cautiously
around the large boulder behind which he had fallen.

In his panic and haste to out run his enemies,
Jasper had made no attempt to cover his trail and the
Indians burst from the forest and spilled out onto the
rock slide at the same point where he had and stopped
to survey the mountain side.   They could find no
sign of their highly prized prey and it was obvious to
Jasper that they were momentarily confused at
having lost him.

With any luck at all, he thought, they'll give up
and go on back home.

Fifty yards below him, the Blackfeet knew there was only one way the hated white man could have gone, and that was up. With much talk and many gestures they began the arduous climb to the top. It was not over yet, and Jasper Pughsey knew it.

This is goin' ta be one bad time an' if'n I ain't goin' under, now's the time ta do somethin' about it, Jasper thought. This child's gettin' purely mad at all this inconvenience. Allus we did was set out fer some hump ribs and I've had m' bell rung, been tied up all night, and nearly had the insides run outta me. That's it, that's all, I've plumb had enough.

Slowly Jasper raised the big Hawkin to his shoulder, drawing a bead on the nearest Blackfoot thirty yards down the steep hillside. He held the huge rifle to his shoulder and cheek as if it were the dearest thing in his life and slowly squeezed the trigger. The long rifle jumped violently as a puff of black smoke billowed from its percussion lock. The half-ounce ball struck the nearest Indian squarely in the chest lifting him a good three feet off the gound and throwing him violently down the rocky talus. His companions ducked behind any available rock in reaction to their confederate's violent end. Hurridly, Jasper recharged the giant Hawkin and took careful aim down the apparently vacant rock slide.

As if by signal several Indians scurried from their hiding places and droped behind rocks further up the slope. As they dropped from sight, three or four more skittered up the slope and disappeared behind cover. Others began the same movement.

So that's their game, Jasper thought. Well I saw ya drap right 'bout there. He took careful aim at the rock behind which the nearest Indian had

dropped from sight. As the Blackfoot sprang for the
next secure place in the rocks, Jasper pulled the
trigger knocking the Indian back down the slope into
two of his companions who had jumped up to follow.
With savage screams the remaining Blackfeet
braves arose as one and began rapidly climbing
toward the white devil at the top of the mountain.

"That's it," Jasper said aloud to himself, "they
ain't takin' this child without more trouble than
that."

Knowing that he had no time to reload the
Hawkin, Jasper put his back to the large boulder
behind which he had been hiding, jammed his heels
into the surrounding rocks and began to heave. He
could hear the Blackfoot braves nearing the top of the
rock slide and began to wonder if he should take off
on another dead run, but he had unmistakably felt
the huge rock move. Again, he strained against the
boulder and it rocked precariously out over the slide.
Jasper tried again with all he had and the boulder
began to move, slowly teetering at first and then,
over the edge and down the steep slide. As the
awkward giant began to move, it started other rocks
moving with it and the entire slide began to move
with a deep, frightening rumble, drowning out the
screams of the Blackfeet as they became engulfed in
the roaring, tumbling rubble.

Jasper stood on the edge of the ridge and was
quickly engulfed in a choking cloud of dust. The
whole mountain shook until the mountain man
nearly lost his footing. His growing satisfaction at
defeating so vicious an enemy at such impossible
odds knew no bounds.

Jasper began to chuckle, "There's gonna be
whailin' in that camp t'nigh...wha..."

Out of the dark cloud of dust arose a giant Blackfoot brave. He appeared like an aparition, his arm held high above his head, a gleaming knife gripped in his fist. Jasper had no time to think, he simply reacted by reaching up and grabbing the brave's wrist, jamming his foot in the Indian's belly, and wrenching backwards. The big Indian was too heavy to throw and the two mortal enemies slammed to the earth. Locked in a violent struggle, they rolled in the rocks at the edge of the precipice. With a single thrust the huge Indian pitched Jasper on his back. The Blackfoot was unbelievably strong, but as they struggled face to face, Jasper held the Indian's wrist high above their heads. The Indian's other hand grasped Jasper's throat and began to close tight. The mountain man fought for breath but none came and the tumbling world began to fade into black. Bright orange blobs began to explode in the darkness of his mind

Jasper's free hand grasped wildly in the grass as he fought to maintain consciousness. Grasping a handful of dirt, the mountain man threw it into the face of the Blackfoot brave. The Indian screamed and tore his hand loose in a futile effort to claw the dirt from his eyes. Jasper's lungs filled with deep gasps of air and with what strength he could muster he arched his back, throwing the momentarily disabled brave off of his body.

The Blackfoot rolled in the dirt trying to rub the grit from his eyes and struggled blindly to his feet at the edge of the precipice. Clutching his crushed throat and gasping for air, Jasper struggled to his feet. His vision slowly clearing, the mountain man saw his assailant staggering on the edge of the steep rock slide. With one kick, he sent the brave over the edge and turned and ran to the opposite side of the ridge. Below him spralled a steep slope of grass broken by loose rock. A hundred yards beyond, the forest sloped steeply to the white waters of a wild river a half mile below.

Jasper Pughsey picked up his Hawkin and descended the mountain.

Though in poor repair and fast crumbling to ruin from disuse, Fort Laramie was an oasis in the wilderness. After fording the North Platt, the small party could see the fort nestled at the foot of some low, rolling hills.

"Is that it...is that Fort Laramie?" asked Jennifer. With the coming of nightfall and overcast skies, only the outlines of a few buildings could be seen in the distance.

"Yep, that's it," replied Obediah Jones. He spoke softly to the two tired horses as he brought the wagon to a stop at the top of a small knoll.

"It's not much to look at, but it'll be home to us for a few days. Besides, it's the safest place around and that's what we need right now, a place to lay low until Jasper and Butch catch up with us."

Obediah had no sooner mentioned Butch's name that he wished he hadn't.

Deborah's eyes misted over. "Are they going to catch up?"

"They should have caught up with us by now, don't you think, Mr. Jones," asked Jennifer anxiously.

"I've told you two not to worry. Butch is with Jasper, and there isn't anything he can't handle.

And if you don't believe me, just ask him when he gets here."

To forestall any further anxiety about Butch, and questions he could not answer, Obediah Jones flipped the reins along the backs of the horses. "Get up...the sooner ya get us there, the sooner you can rest."

The two tired animals slowly responded and the wagon rolled off of the low hill and on toward the welcome fort.

Obediah brought the wagon to a halt between two small adobe buildings. "Halloo," he called. Only the echo of his voice answered him. "Strange...I'd have thought Bordeaux would be here, or at least one of his men."

"What a lonely place," commented Jennifer, as she wearily climbed down from the wagon. "There's nobody here, then?"

"There doesn't appear to be," responded Obediah. They must be out hunting or maybe there's something going on somewhere around here...parlay with some Indians or something."

"It's certainly not what I expected a fort to look like," said Deborah."

Obediah had begun unhitching the animals. "And what exactly were you expecting?" he asked.

Well," said Deborah, "I thought it would have a big wooden wall around it with big towers at each corner and a massive gate that would keep out hostile Indians and all."

"Well, I'm sorry you're disappointed," Obediah said, stripping harness from the backs of the two horses.

"Oh, it's not that, exactly....

"What's it used for, Mr. Jones," Jennifer interjected.

"Nothing now, really...some trading...but believe me this place had its day in the sun."

"It did?"

"Yep...Jasper and I have spent many a wild time here with Indians and other traders."

"Really...what did you do?" asked Jennifer, her insatiable interest growing.

Obediah climbed into the back of the wagon. "You girls come and get this cooking gear and this meat. Nothing will do for right now like a good hot meal. I'm nearly starved to death."

Jennifer climbed up on the wagon's left front wheel and began handing cooking materials and food down to Deborah. "Tell us about this place, Mr. Jones."

"Let me picket the horses out in that grass and get some wood so you two can start dinner and we'll talk some."

After picketing the horses a short distance from the wagon, Obediah Jones gathered wood and buffalo chips and returned to camp.

"Where'll we build the fire, Mr. Jones?" asked Jennifer.

"Well, there's no need to do it out here," he said. I can see my breath already. It's going to be a cold night and it's probably going to snow. Gather up your stuff. There's a fireplace in that adobe building over there, if I remember correctly."

"Oh, that's wonderful," responded Deborah. "A roof over our heads and a fire place."

"After all we've been through, it somehow won't seem natural," said Jennifer.

"Natural or not, let's do it," said Obediah, ducking through the low door.

The mountain man dropped the material for the fire at the side of a small fireplace in the far wall of the narrow room. A pack rat had accumulated a cache of string, straw, cloth, and other material in the fireplace. "Looks occupied," said the mountain man. "Whoever the little critter was that did all this work has my gratitude, though. He has made it a lot easier to get a fire going."

Obediah stacked some twigs and small branches in the fireplace and in a very short time fire curled hungrily around the wood.

"Oh," said Deborah, "this is going to be nice. Just look how clean this place is. You'd think someone lived here."

Obediah threw more wood and some chips on the fire and it responded with renewed energy, filling the small room with dim, flickering light.

"Well, besides the traders that live here off and on now, lots of folks have lived here. And some not too long ago."

"Who?" asked Jennifer.

"Well, I expect your people spent a day or two here when they passed through. There are wagon tracks all over the place and fairly fresh animal droppings out in the yard. This is on what is known as the Oregon trail, and people come by here all the time on their way west. Looks to me like there was a bunch here as recently as a week ago, maybe not that long. And a lot of trading still goes on, too."

"Do you think we'll see some folks?"

"Possible...some trappers, maybe. Bordeaux and some of his men, but I doubt if we'll see anyone else. We're going to be out of here in the next day or

two.   We've got some awfully rugged country
between here and where you want to go and the
weather's not going to hold much longer. In fact, I
don't know if you noticed, but there is a light snow
falling out there right now. It was just starting when
we came in here."

Deborah began filling the pan with meat and
soon the room was filled with the aroma of frying
buffalo steaks. "We'll eat pretty soon. It won't take
long for this meat to cook."

"The sooner, the better," said Obediah Jones,
his stomach rumbling in response.

The fire warmed them and they ate in silence.

"Bit tough," said Obediah, cleaning his plate,
"but it sure hit the spot."

"This place is surely spooky," said Jennifer.
"I'll bet its haunted. Is it haunted, Mr. Jones?"

"A place that has seen as much life as this old
fort has is bound to have some ghosts around.
Especially on a night like this."

"Tell us about Fort Laramie," said Deborah.
"How come you and Mr. Pughsey know it so well?"

Obediah plucked a small twig from the side of
the fire and began picking his teeth. He leaned back
on his elbows and looked into the fire. "For a long
time this old fort saw a lot of business. The trappers
would bring their beaver pelts and other furs in here
to trade for the things they needed to survive in the
mountains."

"Really?"

"Yep. The old place used to be known as Fort
John. It was owned for a long time by the American
Fur Company and it was a major trading center here
on the eastern slope of the Rocky Mountains."

"A major trading center? You mean it was that busy way out here?" Jennifer asked with suprise.

"It's hard to imagine, I guess. Bands of Cheyennes, Arapahoes, and Sioux would camp all around here and trade their pelts and robes for dry goods, beads, tobacco, and whiskey."

"Did you and Mr. Pughsey come here often?" Deborah asked.

"Quite often. It was a wild time when we mountain men and all those Indians would get together. The worst thing you can give an Indian—any Indian—is whiskey. They don't get drunk like a white man, they just go plain crazy."

"Well, why give it to them then?" asked Deborah.

"Oh, for two reasons, l guess. First off, there is no wilder bunch than the mountain men. They love a good time, and the wilder it is, the better they like it. The only thing a mountain man likes better than a good fight is an outright brawl, and drunk Indians will provide the action faster than just about anything I can think of."

"What's the other reason?" asked Jennifer.

"Well, it's easier to cheat them out of their goods and their women."

"Oh...my," said Deborah.

"Sorry...I didn't mean to..."

"Why cheat them, Mr. Jones?" asked Jennifer. "That's not fair."

"Out here survival is what counts, and that's all that counts. So it seems to be every man for himself in more ways than one, unfortunately. The more moccasins you can get in a trade, the further and more comfortably you can walk. So you get as many as you can for as little as possible." Obediah studied his feet as they warmed by the fire. "In fact, that's how I got these."

"Did you get them here?" asked Jennifer.

"Nope. I got these a few weeks ago up at Pierre's Hole...before we found you. It's quite a ways north of here; many days ride, in fact. The point is, you either get them by trading or you buy them, and that can get awfully expensive."

"Expensive?" asked Deborah, incredulously. "Mocassins? Made of skin? How much do they cost?"

"Well out here they can cost as much as a dollar a pair, and so can a good lariat."

"Well, why do they cost so much for what you get?"

"Well," Obediah responded, "if you're going to live out in the Great Basin wilderness, there are some things you ought to keep in mind. It's not like it was back where you come from; things—important things—are different. First of all, there is very little money floating around out here. It's awfully hard to get your hands on any, so you have to barter. In other words, you have to give something of value to a squaw—something she wants or needs—before you can get a pair of moccasins out of her. Secondly, nobody out here is in the business of making shoes or boots. That means that moccasins are highly prized, because that's about all you can get. Besides, for the way a mountain man has to live, moccasins are by far superior to a pair of boots or shoes. They are light and quiet, and that's important. And things like sugar or coffee or spices can really get expensive."

Obediah walked over to the door and watched the snow fall for a moment. "Tomorrow, I'm going to find Butch and Jasper. If we're going to make it to the Great Basin, we've got to get going."

"But what will we do?" asked Jennifer.

"You two will stay right here. You'll be safe enough. Besides, Bordeaux or some of his men will likely be back."

"But what about Indians? Aren't there Indians around here?" asked Deborah.

"A few, but they'll be peaceful enough. If you see any, they'll probably be Cheyennes. They are a very clean and civilized people. Just treat them like you would anyone else and you'll have no problems. Anyway, I'll be back before you know it. In fact, those two might just walk in on us during the night.

"Keep the fire going. I'm going to sleep out in the wagon," Obediah Jones said, ducking through the low door and disappearing into the cold night.

Grunt pushed aside a large, fragrant branch of juniper and walked out onto a rocky outcropping overlooking a large sunken meadow surrounded by the forest. Butch followed close behind the large, redolent Indian. The two stopped and surveyed the wild beauty spread beneath them.

"Gee," said the boy, "I've never seen a place 's beautiful as out here in these mountains."

"Ugnh," responded the big Indian, pointing down into the grassy basin beneath them.

"Huh?" Butch said, looking in the general direction of the Indian's pointing finger. "What? I don't see nothin'. Gosh, I wish Mr. Pughsey were here."

"Ugnh," Grunt said more urgently pulling the boy's head closer to his pointing arm.

Butch squirmed from the Indian's grasp. "What, I don't...holy cow, what is it...it's a bear, and it must be a big one, too. Just look at it...holy cow."

The large bear was slowly lumbering along the edge of a small stream which wound among the willows and grass down in the meadow.

The boy started down the broken slope toward the meadow. "Let's go look."

"Ugnh," Grunt responded, grabbing the boy by the neck of his shirt and waiving his other hand in a negative gesture. The Indian pointed around the basin to the left and gave the boy a shove in that direction.

Butch scrambled clumsily over some rocks in an effort to find a path around the basin in the direction Grunt had pointed. "But...I don't see why..."

"Ugnh," Grunt snarled viciously.

"Huh?" Butch turned to see Grunt towering over him, his arms held above his head, his hands clawing the air.

Butch stepped back. "Oh...yeah...I guess they're pretty mean, huh?"

"Ugnh," responded the big Indian shaking his head vigorously and gesturing for Butch to move on around the meadow.

Taking the lead, the big Indian led the boy down the hillside and into the meadow downstream from where they had seen the bear. The grass was deep and smelled sweet to the two weary travelers as they made their way to the edge of the clear mountain creek. The water ran slowly, forming large, deep pools. Small bugs skated among the autumn leaves that floated on the surface and large fish could be seen swimming near the bottom. Butch and Grunt lay down on the damp, mossy bank and drank deeply of the cool, green water.

Butch thought he had never tasted anything quite so delicious in all of his life. He buried his head in the pool, the cold water gurgling in his submerged ears, and watched the large fish waving gracefully in the slow current on the bottom. His face began to ache from the icy water. Butch pulled his head from the pool, vigorously shook the water from his face and hair, and looked squarely into two pair of large, inquisitive brown eyes watching him closely across the small stream.

Slowly, so as not to frighten the two grizzly cubs, Butch reached over and shook Grunt's arm. "Grunt...lookit...Grunt?"

While Butch had buried his head in the water, Grunt had rolled over on the damp bank and lay staring into the deep, blue sky. As un-characteristic of him as it was, he had not heard the two cubs as they had appeared on the opposite bank.

The cubs were frozen in fascination as they watched the two strangers on the opposite bank. Slowly, one of the cubs rose up on his hind feet and began to bawl loudly, and soon the other joined in the chorus.

"Ugnh." Grunt quickly grabbed Butch, pulled him to his feet, and shoved him harshly down stream, gesturing for him to run.

In an effort to get his balance, Butch slipped and fell over the side of the bank and slid up to his knees in the cold water. "Yeow!" he hollered, as he scrambled back up onto the muddy bank.

In reaction to the confusion on the opposite bank, both cubs dropped on all four paws and, bawling loudly, scampered into the bushes and willows behind them.

A few yards out in the meadow the huge she grizzly rose on her back legs to her full eight feet in height in an effort to discover the the apparent danger to her two cubs who were scrambling through the bushes toward their mother.

Butch heard the mother grizzly's angry growls and his legs began moving faster than they had ever moved before. Butch began to feel as if he were flying, his feet touching the ground so briefly and lightly that he could hardly feel the impact. He knew, however, that he was not moving nearly fast enough, because Grunt kept grabbing him by the seat of his pants and boosting him ahead in short, but frequent, bursts of even greater speed.

With a roar and a swat the huge grizzly sent her two errant cubs scampering toward the safety of a tree at the edge of the meadow, then turned in blind rage and drove headlong into the brush in pursuit of the fleeing Grunt and Butch. The huge grizzly's rapid, lumbering strides quickly closed the distance.

"Ugnh!" His chest heaving, Grunt yanked the boy to a stop and thrust him high into a large lodge pole pine.

"But Grunt, what...we gotta...cumon..."

"Ugnh!" The Indian poked his large finger in the air toward Butch demanding that he climb higher. Then, he turned with his back to the tree, drew his knife and, with the stoicism of ages, waited for the charging bear. He would do what was necessary to save his friend's, Jasper Pughsey's, boy.

The grizzly lunged to a halt some ten feet in front of the Indian, spraying a cloud of dust, pine needles, and rocks into the clean autumn air. Then the bear rose on its hind legs to its full height. The big animal swayed from side to side as it watched the man braced at the foot of the pine tree. Its huge forepaws jabbed at the air as it began lumbering toward the waiting Indian.

Grunt could smell the stench of the big animal's breath as it shuffled toward him. It was the smell of violent, agonizing death, and the Indian knew it.

Clenching his large knife tightly in both hands, Grunt raised it high over his head and with one, long scream lunged for the mighty bear's exposed chest. The Indian slammed into the bear's furry embrace and buried his knife deep in the towering animal's chest. The bear roared in agony and, seeking to tear the painful assailant from its body, dragged its large, sharp claws across Grunt's back leaving bloody gashes in the Indian's body.

Screaming with pain and exerting all of the strength he had left, Grunt pulled the knife from the bear's chest and raised it high above his head for another lunge, but a stunning blow from the back of the bear's paw knocked the Indian unconscious into the dirt at the foot of the tree.

The bear stood momentarily dazed, blinded by the pain from the wound in its chest. Hunching its enormous shoulders, its gigantic teeth bared in a vicious snarl, the wounded grizzly lurched toward the helpless Grunt.

In an effort to divert the bear's attention, Butch began hollering at the top of his lungs and shaking the pine tree. The bear stopped and looked at Butch high up in the tree. She slowly lifted one huge forepaw toward Butch, almost reaching the boy's foot. Suddenly, the nearest branch exploded violently into splinters and fell to the earth at the startled bear's feet. The huge bear dropped to all four feet and lumbered off into the forest. At the edge of the meadow Butch saw a white puff of smoke drifting from the lock of Jasper Pughsey's Hawkin.

Butch climbed from the tree and ran across the meadow to meet his great, good friend, the mountain man Jasper Pughsey.

"Mr. Pughsey...Grunt's..."

"I know, boy...maybe I shoulda kilt thet bar, but she's got younguns and it didn't appear needful." Let's go look after Grunt. Seems he needs our help fer once."

After cleaning Grunt's wounds with cold water from the stream, Jasper covered them with a poultice made from moss and dobbed each wound with some of the primitive medicine.

"Looks ta me like Old Ephraim got the best a you two," said Jasper.

"Who's Old Ephraim?"

"Oh...boy. Seem's like I'm always explainin' things..."

"Well, if you mean that ol' bear, she ain't feelin' none too good right now either," Butch said, hotly.

Jasper stood up and stretched. "And exactly why's that?"

Well...ol' Grunt jumped into that bear like you wouldn't believe and stabbed 'im good with his

knife. That ol' bear knew she was stuck good, too.
You shoulda heard 'er holler."

"Tell me, young'n...does that ol' she bear look
as bad as poor ol' Grunt here?"

"Well...I guess it's pretty hard t'tell, but I'll just
bet she ain't feelin' none too good either, though."

Jasper stood up. "Now boy, you stay here and be
sure ol' Grunt don't move none if he wakes up. I
don't suppose he will fer a while. Looks ta me like
Old Ephraim really rung his bell."

Butch's eyes began to fill with tears. "Mr.
Pughsey...ol' Grunt's gonna be all right, ain't he?"

"Now, don't go cloudin' up on me, boy. Us
mountain men gotta keep our wits about us at a time
like this." Jasper scratched his chin. "Yew ken be
sure that ol' beaver's seen a lot worse than this.
Grunt's as tough as old leather, and it'll take a lot
bigger bear than that one t' put him under. Give 'im
a little time and he'll be up as mean an' ugly as ever,
mark my words."

"What'er we gonna do now? That old she bear
might decide t' come back and finish us all" said
Butch.

"If she's as hurt as ya say, she'll be off lickin'
her wounds just like we're doin'. What we gotta do
now is get ol' Grunt over to Fort Laramie, and that
might take some doin'."

"How're we gonna do that. He's pretty heavy."

Jasper drew his Green River from its scabbard
and walked over to two small lodge pole pine trees.
"We're gonna make a travois outta these two little
trees and I'm gonna drag 'im. He ain't fit ta walk
or he'll start bleedin' again and we gotta get 'm
where we can take better care of 'im."

The mountain man cut the two small trees and trimmed all of the branches from each trunk. Taking his buckskin shirt off, he tucked each sleeve through the neck opening and ran the two poles through them, creating a makeshift travois. Jasper and Butch pulled the big Indian onto the travois, lifted two ends of the poles to Jasper's shoulders, and started for Fort Laramie. Grunt lay on his stomach draped over the two poles, his head hanging between them, and his feet dragging along the ground behind the laboring Jasper Pughsey.

"Fetch ma Hawkin, boy. We got us a ways t' go."

"Yessir "

Chapter 17

The morning air was bitter cold on the high plateau. Obediah Jones leaned lazily over the saddle horn and watched Jasper Pughsey pulling Grunt on a make-shift travois across the shallow, narrow valley below, the boy trailing along a few paces behind. Obediah's horse stomped and blew and their breath swirled out in front of their faces in billowy, white clouds in the bright morning sun light.

Well, he thought, at least they seem to be in one piece, and are headed in the right direction.

The mountain man dismounted, tied his horse to a nearby pine tree, and sat down on a large rocky outcropping to watch the spectacle of Jasper Pughsey pulling the massive Grunt up the mountain toward him. Jasper's complaints could be clearly heard in the crisp mountain air.

"Dadblamed Indian," he said, straining to lift the travois supports from his sholder and set the two poles on the ground. "What'd he have to go get mauled by a grizzly for, anyhow? Wagh."

"We didn't seem ta have much choice, Mr. Pughsey. That ol' bear ran faster than almost anything I've ever seen before," said Butch, sitting down on the ground next to Grunt.

Jasper knelt on the ground next to his prostrate friend and began examining the big Indian's wounds. "Well, ya certainly learned an important lesson this time, boy. Bears, especially a Grizzly, ain't nothin' ta play with, are they?"

"No, sir."

"An' no matter what, ya don't never fool around a couple of cubs, and it don't matter what kind they are. Their mothers just plain don't like it. That's about the fastest way I can think of ta wind up like poor ol' Grunt here." Jasper removed some of the poultice from Grunt's back and grimaced. "He sure is clawed up bad, ain't he, boy?"

"Yessir...he sure is."

"Well...the best we kin do fer this ol' hoss, is get 'im ta Fort Laramie where he can rest and heal. But it'd surely be easier if he'd jest come to," Jasper said, leaning down and pulling the two braces and their heavy load to his shoulders. "Gimme a hand with this, boy. I gotta get 'em up on my shoulders like before."

"Yessir."

Jasper settled the heavy poles over his shoulders, gripped them tightly near his ears, and began the hard pull up the slope ahead of them.

"Oh...my stars, but this hurts," he complained as he strained to keep his footing on the hill side.

"How much further do ya figger we gotta go, Mr. Pughsey?"

"Well, seems like we've come quite a pace, and if I recollect correctly, and I usually do, oncet we get over this here hill it's only a mile 'r two ta the fort. Wagh."

Jasper strained hard, the steep hillside and the weight of his big Indian friend pulling the two rough poles from his sore hands.

"I think maybe I better set 'im down fer a minute," Jasper said, straining to gain his breath. "This here's a tougher climb than I thought it'd be."

"Don't set 'im there Jasper. He might roll all the way back down the hill and then you'd have to just pull him all the way back up again," hollered Obediah Jones from his perch on a large rock near the top of the hill.

"Wha..." the startled Jasper Pughsey looked up to see Obediah a few yards ahead of him. "Yew like ta scared the pants off'n me, Obediah Jones."

"Well, I had to speak up or you likely would have pulled that mighty fine travios right over me. I didn't mean ta startle ya," Obediah said, getting to his feet and brushing the dirt from the seat of his pants.

"Get that horse down here and help me get this thing ta the top. How long yew been there anyways?" hollered Jasper Pughsey.

Obediah walked over and untied his horse and led it down the hill to where Jasper had laid the poles of the travios on the ground. "Well, I figured you'd be coming this way so I've just been sitting here waiting for you. I guess I've been watching your magnificent struggle for about the past hour, now."

Obediah backed the horse into a position where the poles of the travois could be secured to the saddle horn. "There's absolutely nothing this man can't do. Right, Butch?"

"Yessir...I mean...no sir," said the exhausted boy." I jest gotta sit down fer a minute. Seems like we've been walkin' an awful long time."

The two men lifted the two ends of the travois over the horse's rump and crossed them over the saddle horn. Using a leather thong, Jasper Pughsey

secured them tightly. Thus secured, the poles passed
on each side of the horse's rump and down to the
ground a few feet behind the animal. The still
unconscious Grunt lay suspended on the travois
between the animal's behind and the ground.

"Mosta the night, in fact," Jasper said. "With
you a settin up here admirin' the scenery, ol' Grunt
here coulda died. In fact, we all coulda died."

"Well," said Obediah, in self defense, "I
haven't been here all that long. I just got here as you
started up the hill. Besides, I know how you hate to be
interfered with when you've started a project with
such determination. So, I thought I'd better stay here
just in case you needed my help, and it never seemed
like you did. So, I just waited until you got here.
Seemed like the natural thing to do at the time. I
guess I don't understand why you're so upset."

Obediah Jones knew all of Jasper Pughsey's
sore spots and he knew just how to massage them on
every occasion.

"Oh, you don't," responded Jasper, hotly.
"Well, let me tell ya..."

"Mr. Jones...have we got much farther ta go?"
Butch interjected. "I'm gettin' awful tired."

"Come here, son," Obediah said, lifting the boy
to his feet. "You look plum tuckered out. I guess
you've had quite an adventure with old Jasper, huh?"

"Yessir."

"Well, let's put you right up here in the saddle
where you can watch the bindings of the travois and
tell us if they start to come loose. Here...put your foot
in the stirrup," the mountain man said, giving the
tired boy a boost. "If we get started now," he said,
looking at Jasper Pughsey, "and stop all of this

palaver, we ought to be back at the fort in time for a
big dinner with your sisters. How does that sound?"

"Yessir...it sure sounds good to me."

Butch ran through the low door of the adobe
building and out into the open compound of Fort
Laramie.

"Mr. Pughsey...Mr. Pughsey...Grunt's gone
an' we can't find 'im nowhere."

"Gone, ya say." Jasper pushed past the boy and
ducked into the small room. Both girls were
hurridly finishing their dressing.

"He must have left last night," said Deborah.
"When we awakened a few minutes ago, he wasn't
here."

"Where could he be?" asked Jennifer,
breathlessly pulling her last shoe on.

Jasper walked over to the corner where they had
laid the unconscious Grunt when they had returned
to the fort the evening before.

"Well...I can't rightly say," he said scratching
his grizzled chin. "But m' guess is that he's gone
back to his people where he can get some proper care
for his back. Them Indians gotta cure fer jest about
anything what ails ya."

"But he was so sick..."

"Don't go wastin' yer worry on ol' Grunt.
He'll be all right. That old beaver knows what he's
doin'. And besides, he's done this afore. He's
always sneakin' off an' then showin' up when ya
least expect 'im, but need 'im the most...usually."

Jasper walked to the door and turned. "You
ladies fix some vittles as quick as ya can. We'll

leave as soon as we've et. Now ol' Grunt's gone, there ain't no need ta hang around here. The trip's gonna be a lot rougher from here on and we best make tracks. Cummon, Butch, us men got work t' do afore we can get on our way."

Jasper Pughsey, with Butch following in his footsteps, walked across the yard to the corral where they found Obediah Jones giving the two big horses the last of their hay.

Obediah Jones looked up from his work. "He's gone, huh?"

"Yep...jest like always."

"I wonder when we'll see him next."

"Likely not too soon. I think things is gettin' too crowded around these parts fer 'im. I'm inclined to agree," said Jasper.

"I know the feeling. Bordeaux was telling me that the traffic was getting heavy along the trail, what with the Mormons and all."

"A lot of 'em, huh?"

"That's what he said."

"Say...that gives me an idee." Jasper turned to find Butch setting on the corral fence listening to the two men. "Butch...run t' the wagon an' fetch the harness an' all, will ya?"

"Yessir." The boy jumped from the pole fence and was gone.

Jasper scratched his bald spot. "What with all the troubles we been havin', I been thinkin' some about Saint Louie an' New Orleans and all a the pleasures this life can hold fer a couple a savvy he coons like us."

"Well," Obediah responded, placing his pitchfork back inside the rough, wooden lean-to attached to the building adjoining the corral, "me, too. But doesn't it seem to you that we've got a bit of a problem right now. These kids are pretty dependent upon us, aren't they?"

"Why, sure. But it's like ol' Bordeaux tol' ya, there's wagons along here all the time. Mormons come through here regular like."

"So, that's how your stick floats, huh?"

"Well...I..."

"You really think it's that simple, Jasper?"

"Well...now...I..."

"Hold on, here comes Butch. Do you really want that boy to hear you talking this way?"

"Oh...now look...I didn't..."

Butch appeared around the corner of the nearest building with an arm full of heavy harness dragging behind him in the dust.

Jasper grabbed the harness and said, "Butch, let's see how fast we can git these here horses bridled and ready to go. You get on the other side there and we'll git this harness on and you kin take the horses out and hitch 'em t' the wagon."

"Yessir," the boy responded eagerly.

As the two worked to untangle all of the leather straps and harness Buck and Nails together, Jasper Pughsey watched the boy. Butch worked enthusiastically and jumped to meet Jasper's every instruction. That young'n is all right, he thought. He's fallered me through all kinds a trouble and he still acts like I got every answer. Still, he thought guiltily, me and Obediah could find some a those pork eaters headin' west that'd let these kids tag along. It ain't that far now, anyways.

"How's that, Mr. Pughsey?"

Jasper jumped from his reverie. "Looks jest fine, boy."

"That boy's the ha'r of the b'ar, Jasper," said Obediah, patting Nails on his broad rump and straightening some harness around the horse's tail. "Take them out and hitch them to the wagon, Butch."

"Yessir...cummon...hup," said the boy, flipping the reins along the backs of the two big horses. Dust rose into the morning air as the big animals and the boy moved out of the corral and around the corner of the building toward the wagon waiting in the yard.

As soon as the boy was out of sight Obediah turned to his friend and said, "It's not all that simple Jasper. We've got a bit of an obligation here. We started out to get these kids to the basin of the Great Salt Lake and I don't think we should let them down now. Isn't that right?"

"Well...I..."

"Look, we'll be there before you know it. We'll head on up river to Devil's Gate, then on back up the Sweetwater to South Pass, over the divide and down to Bridger, and from there we'll make good..."

"Wagons! Wagons!" came an excited cry from somewhere out in the compound of the fort.

Obediah and Jasper turned and ran from the corral out into the yard as one of Brodeaux's men, twisting in his saddle and pointing to his rear, galloped by and reined the horse to a stop in a cloud of dust at the door of the building used by the great trapper. Bordeaux appeared in the doorway and soon others gathered in the yard. Ten or fifteen wagons could be seen rolling toward the fort, clouds of dust swirling from their wheels.

"Tarnation," said Jasper, slapping his knee, "I'll bet ya ma prize pelts them's more Mormons right now. Why, I'll bet them young'ns got friends and family in that bunch right there."

"Jasper," responded Obediah, "we found them where we did because their family had been killed."

The wagons slowly pulled into the open compound of the fort and pulled in a large half circle in front of the main buildings. The women and children of the large group began milling around the entire area as the men assembled loosely in front of Bordeaux's door. Jasper and Obediah walked over near the group where they could hear the men talking of their troubles. One of them, a big, unshaven man dressed in a faded red under shirt which buttoned down the middle and a pair of worn-out cotton pants held up by dirty, wide suspenders, stepped forward and addressed Bordeaux.

"We all from Illinois and Missoura an' headed for the Oregon territory," he drawled, "an' we're a might in need of some supplies." It was obvious to the two mountain men that the man and some of his companions had been drinking.

"A wonder they got this far," grumbled Jasper.

As Bordeaux stepped out into the yard and began explaining to the group how scarce supplies were, Obediah Jones took Jasper by the sleeve and gestured him away from the crowd. The two began walking toward the building that for the past few days had been home to them and Richards' children.

"See, Jasper. These people are not only not Mormons, they just might be some of the very people that's caused them so much trouble."

Jasper turned and again surveyed the motly group. "Yew think maybe they...naw..."

"Well, now, ya can't be too sure, can ya. They aren't the most savory looking bunch and half of them are near drunk right now."

"I'd say so...kinda stink a bit, don't they," Jasper agreed.

As Obediah and Jasper approached the building they had occupied with the Richards children, Deborah and Jennifer stepped out into the yard.

"Look at all of the people," said Jennifer with an enthusiasm she had not felt in a very long time.

"I wonder where they're from," said Deborah.

"Do you think they're some of us?" asked Jennifer excitedly, as she started across the compound toward the group of strangers.

"Jennifer," hollered Obediah Jones, "why don't you come over here with us? We need to be leaving."

"I'll be right back," she hollered over her shoulder, "I just want to see who they are."

"She'll be all right," said Deborah, turning and reentering the adobe building.

"Well...I really think we should..."

"Yer a regalar old woman, Obediah Jones. Ain't one chance in a million she'd know any a them, anyways," Jasper chided.

Jennifer ran up to the crowd as the man in the faded red undershirt turned from his brief talk with Boredauex and began pushing his way roughly through the group of men that had followed him from their wagons. He was angry from Bordeaux's refusal to give him all of the supplies he demanded. Jennifer almost bumped into him.

"Get outta my way ya clumsy..."

"Oh...I'm sorry..."

"Hey," he said, grabbing her roughly by her blouse, "don't I know you?"

The man known as Hawky swayed and blinked from the bright sun and held the girl tightly by her shoulder. She could smell his dirty clothes and his breath was strong with the smell of homemade whisky.

"Answer me, gal...I'm talkin' t' ya..."

Frightened, Jennifer began to pull from his grip. "No...I...please, you're hurting..."

"Why...yer one a them no good Mormon brats what sold me that no good cow...I outta pull..."

Climbing from the wagon Butch saw the man grab Jennifer and jerk her toward him. "Hey...mister," he hollered as he jumped from the wagon and ran across the yard. "You better let her go."

The big man turned as Butch ran up and kicked him in the shin of one of his legs as hard as he could. The man yelled out with pain and letting go of Jennifer and dancing on one foot, he grabbed Butch by his hair and nearly yanked the boy off of his feet.

"You dirty little..."

Butch yelled from the man's painful hold.

The big Missourian was cut short as Jasper Pughsey's large fist caught him squarely in the mouth, mashing his lips and lifting him off of the ground. The big ruffian fell flat on his back in the dirt. Dazed, the man wiped blood from his crushed mouth and struggled to his feet as the unfriendly group began to close around them.

"You want to finish the job, Jasper? Or maybe the gentleman would prefer to go his way, no more said," yelled Obediah from the doorway. His long rifle indiscriminately surveyed the crowd from his shoulder. "Someone tries something funny and someone gets hurt. It's that simple."

"From this way, too." Bordeaux stood in the doorway of his trading store, his buffalo rifle held loosely at his hip. "And, my friends, just look around you. Much foolishness will bring much trouble, no?" Ten armed men seemed to have appeared from nowhere.

"Back to your wagons, eh?" The trader made small circles in the dusty air with the tip of his large rifle. "It is best we stop this now."

Jasper stepped back allowing some space between them. "I ever see you so much as look at one a these young'ns again an' I'll lift your dirty, stinkin' scalp," he said, poking at the man's chest. "You savvy? I'll wear your hair on m' belt."

"Them damn kids..."

Jasper stepped toward the man, his Green River knife appearing in his hand from nowhere. "No more, mister...not one more word outta yer drunkun mouth."

The big man's shoulders sagged. "You win fer now," he said. "But there'll be other times." In spite of his effort to regain some dignity, he was defeated. He knew it, the mountain man that confronted him knew it, and what was worse, all of his people knew it.

"Let's go Obediah. We gotta get these kids t' their people. Ain't no one else can do it. Wagh!"

The next week went by uneventfully. With four new horses which Obediah had purchased from Bordeaux, the traveling was much easier. One man would drive the wagon pulled by Buck and Nails and the others each had a horse to ride. They made rapid progress, though the weather was beginning to deteriorate as autumn moved into the high country. On several occasions they ran into Missourians on their way west to Oregon, but Obediah and Jasper kept their party to themselves and except for one or two short inquiries from other travelers about weather and directions, there were no encounters. When other groups of pioneers were sighted, Jasper would grumble, "We don't want no truck with them pork eaters," and they would move on to more secluded camp sites. On several occasions, as they slowly made their way up the divide toward South Pass, they sighted wooden markers left by an earlier group of Mormon pioneers which indicated that the Mormons had passed this way. Each marker contained an estimate of how much progress had been made from Fort Laramie.

"It makes me feel good just to see that marker, and all of the others we've seen, too," said Deborah.

"Why is that?" asked Obediah.

"Because our people have come this way. I'm glad we camped here. I feel close to them."

Jasper and Butch walked up to them and Jasper said, "Ain't gonna be long now, young lady. We'll soon be there, though ya shouldn't expect too much when ya get there."

"I don't care what it's like. It's where the Lord wants us."

"Mebbe." Talk of the Lord always made the old mountain man a little uneasy.

"Whadda ya mean we'll soon be there, Mr. Pughsey?" asked Butch.

"Come here," he said, leading the group up the hillside to the top of the ridge, a few hundred yards from their evening camp.

"Oh, will you just look at that," said Deborah, with wonder.

"Oh...it's...beautiful," said Jennifer.

The sun was setting in a glory of red and purple sky. The large clouds softly piled above the mountains were white and edged with bright gold. It was cold and the air was clean. Deep snow banks lay in the shaded areas. To each of the weary travelers it suddenly seemed good to be alive to enjoy such beauty, even when enjoyed at such enormous personal cost.

Obediah filled his lungs with the cold air and slowly let it out. "I guess that's why Jasper and I could never leave this wild country. Isn't that right old hoss?"

"Reckon it is at that," said Jasper, his voice filled with a deep emotion. "Trouble is, it's changin'. I reckon good things jest can't last."

"How's it changin', Mr. Pughsey," asked Butch.

"People, that's how. Mormons, Missourians, an' who knows what's next. Won't be no room left fer a man ta breathe."

For a long time the group fell silent and then Jasper shook himself from his reverie. "See where the land rises to a kind of wide saddle yonder?"

"I see it," said Butch.

"Well, young'n, thet's the South Pass of the Rocky Mountains."

"It is?"

"Yep. The great divide. Some folks don't hardly notice it, it seems sa gradual. But that's the continental divide."

"What does that mean?" Asked Jennifer.

"That means that when we cross over it in the mornin', all the rivers on t'other side run to the west, 'sted a the east?"

"No kiddin'?" asked Butch.

"That's right," said Obediah. "We've reached the spine of the continent. This is sort of like the ridge line of the entire country."

The sun was almost gone and it was getting dark. The cold was settling over the tired travelers like a chilled blanket.

"Best we get back to camp," said Obediah. "Tomorrow's going to get here early and we've got to move on. We don't want to be caught in these mountains when the real snow starts."

Obediah and the two girls started back to camp.

"We'll be along," Jasper hollered. Turning to Butch he said, "Us men gotta do some contemplatin."

"Yeah," said Butch.

The old man and the young boy sat down on the cold ground and watched the last golden bow of the sun slide beneath the ragged rim of the earth and blackness settled over the wilderness.

"Mr. Pughsey...are we really gonna make it? Seems like it's been ferever since we left Nauvoo?"

Jasper looked down at the dark outline of the young boy he had come to love. "Son, after all we been through, you an' me t'gether, 'specially, we have made it. Wagh!"

The mountain man unbuckled the belt at his waist and slid the Green River in its fringed buckskin scabbard from it.

"It's time you had one of these," he said handing the treasured knife to the boy.

"Gosh...I..." For the first time in his young life the boy was without adequate words. "I..."

"It's yours, boy. As far as this ol' beaver's concerned, you've earned it. You're a real mountain man."

"Really?"

"Yep. You been up the creek and over the mountain. You're the ha'r of the b'ar, you are. Me an' Obediah's proud ta have ya as a partner."

Butch clutched the treasured Green River tightly in his hands and sat up straight next to his great friend and benefactor. He could hear the great mountain man breathing next to him and feel the smoothness of his buckskin shirt and pants. This was what it was like, the true wilderness, the mountains. The boy's heart swelled with the pride known by all mountain men. He had come to truly know the wilderness and loved its wild, grand, dangerous beauty. Grateful to be where he was, the boy filled his young lungs with the clean, cold mountain air and said, "Wagh!"

THE END

Brad E. Hainsworth received his B.A., M.A., and Ph.D degrees from the University of Utah. His studies were in the field of Political Science and Public Administration.

Dr. Hainsworth's experiences have included being a Staff Assistant to the President of the United States, Assistant Director of the Office of Economic Opportunity, Deputy Assistant Secretary of the Interior for Land and Water Resources, Deputy Lieutenant Governor of the State of Utah. He also taught at several universities including the University of Utah, the University of Montana, and Pepperdine University.

Brad Hainsworth is the author of *Camp of the Saints*, and co-author of *In The Lion's Den; The Story of Senator Orrin Hatch*. Hainsworth is currently a professor of Communications at Brigham Young University.